DINING OUT AT HOME
CALGARY

Served by Myriam Leighton & Jennifer Stead

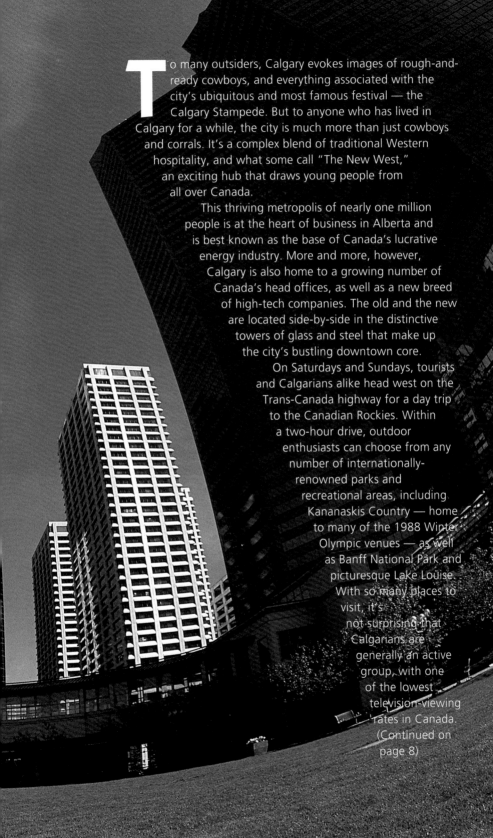

To many outsiders, Calgary evokes images of rough-and-ready cowboys, and everything associated with the city's ubiquitous and most famous festival — the Calgary Stampede. But to anyone who has lived in Calgary for a while, the city is much more than just cowboys and corrals. It's a complex blend of traditional Western hospitality, and what some call "The New West," an exciting hub that draws young people from all over Canada.

This thriving metropolis of nearly one million people is at the heart of business in Alberta and is best known as the base of Canada's lucrative energy industry. More and more, however, Calgary is also home to a growing number of Canada's head offices, as well as a new breed of high-tech companies. The old and the new are located side-by-side in the distinctive towers of glass and steel that make up the city's bustling downtown core.

On Saturdays and Sundays, tourists and Calgarians alike head west on the Trans-Canada highway for a day trip to the Canadian Rockies. Within a two-hour drive, outdoor enthusiasts can choose from any number of internationally-renowned parks and recreational areas, including Kananaskis Country — home to many of the 1988 Winter Olympic venues — as well as Banff National Park and picturesque Lake Louise. With so many places to visit, it's not surprising that Calgarians are generally an active group, with one of the lowest television-viewing rates in Canada.
(Continued on page 8)

Top: *The Pengrowth Saddledome and the Calgary Tower dominate Calgary's skyline*

Bottom: *Devonian Gardens*

Opposite top left: *Reflections of the Calgary Tower*

Opposite top right: *Ski jump at Canada Olympic Park*

Opposite bottom left: *Bovine public art in Calgary*

Opposite bottom right: *Shadows at the Calgary Zoo LRT station*

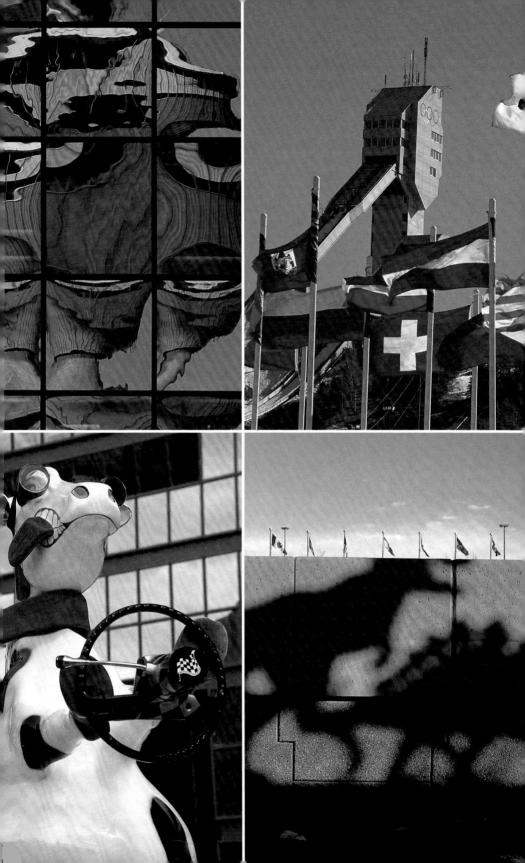

Top: *Conservatory at the Calgary Zoo*

Bottom left: *Celebrating at the Calgary Stampede*

Bottom right: *Monument to Albertans who fought in the South African War (1899-1902)*

Top: *Barrel racing at the Calgary Stampede*

Bottom left: *Horse-drawn wagon in the Stampede parade*

Bottom right: *Rodeo clown*

Heritage Park — 1890s fashion

Although it may seem that Calgary's recent popularity is something new, the truth is, people have been visiting the foothills and the eastern Rockies for 10,000 years. Early residents included the Blackfoot, Blood, Peigan, Sarcee, and Stony peoples, the descendants of whom still make their homes around Calgary. It wasn't until 1873 that the first European settler, Sam Livingston, made his home in the area.

In 1875, soon after Livingston's arrival, the Northwest Mounted Police built Fort Brisbois (later known as Fort Calgary) at the forks of the Bow and Elbow rivers. The burgeoning city was incorporated just a few short years later, in 1894. And between 1908 and 1911 Calgary grew by 30,000 residents, a boom even by today's standards.

In 1912, the wild and woolly Calgary Stampede and Exhibition had its inaugural year. It was in that year that now legendary Tom Three Persons rode Cyclone, the original bucking bronco, wowing crowds and walking away with the princely sum of $1000. For ten days each year, city residents still kick up their heels, chowing down on everything from corn dogs to cotton candy. And while cowboy legends such as Three Persons remain an important part of Calgary's fabric, they do not solely define the city's character. After each Stampede winds down, thousands of pairs of cowboy boots go back on the shelf, and Calgarians set their sights on more sophisticated pursuits.

DINING OUT AT HOME
CALGARY

Served by
Myriam Leighton & Jennifer Stead
Altitude Publishing

DINING OUT AT HOME, CALGARY

Altitude Publishing Canada Ltd.
The Canadian Rockies
1500 Railway Avenue
Canmore, Alberta T1W 1P6
www.altitudepublishing.com
Copyright 2003 © Myriam Leighton and Jennifer Stead

Canadian Cataloguing in Publication Data
Stead, Jennifer
Dining Out at Home, Calgary / Jennifer Stead, Myriam Leighton
(Dining Out at Home)
Includes index.
ISBN 1-55153-930-6

1. Cookery--Alberta--Calgary. 2. Cookery, Canadian--Alberta style.
I. Leighton, Myriam, 1962- II. Title. III. Series: Dining Out at Home. (Canmore, Alta.)
TX715.6.S715 2002   641.597123'38   C2002-911269-9

Project Development

Cover/illustrations	Jennifer Stead
Introduction	Megan Lappi
Photos	Andrew Bradley
Layout	Scott Manktelow
Editing	Kara Turner
Food consulting	Roger McGregor

Altitude GreenTree Program
Altitude Publishing will plant in Canada twice as many trees
as were used in the manufacturing of this product.

Made in Western Canada
Printed and bound in Canada by Friesen Printers, Altona, Manitoba

We acknowledge the financial support of the Government of Canada through the
Book Publishing Industry Development Program (BPIDP) for our publishing activities.

Table of Contents

Preface

With *Dining Out at Home, Calgary*, we offer you a selection of recipes from the creative chefs working in the fine restaurants of this city. We hope that this book will inspire you and add some sparkle to your menus while cooking in the comfort of your own home.

It has been a wonderfully interesting and instructive experience, working with so many fabulous chefs. In gathering the recipes together and presenting the creations of the various chefs, we have tried to stay true to individuals' styles and personal approaches. The result is a mélange of meals from a wide range of restaurants sure to satisfy everyone.

We would like to thank and acknowledge all the exceptional restaurants and chefs for their time and creative generosity, our editors, Roger McGregor and Colleen Dorion, and everyone else who made this possible.

Enjoy!

Myriam and Jennifer

Bonus! Recipe Sampler!

Additional recipes, not included in this book (enough for an entire dinner!) are published on the web. Please visit **www.altitudepublishing.com** and follow the links to Dining Out at Home, Calgary.

Breakfasts

Organic Granola

Serves: 8–10

Part A

2 cups	Rolled oats	500 ml
1 cup	Red River cereal (assorted grain flakes)	250 ml
1/2 cup	Cornmeal	125 ml
1/4 cup	Sunflower seeds	50 ml
1/4 cup	Pumpkin seeds	50 ml
1/4 cup	Assorted nuts (pecans, almonds, hazelnuts)	50 ml
1 tbsp.	Cinnamon	15 ml
1/2 cup	Demerara sugar	125 ml
2 tbsp.	Honey	30 ml
1/4 cup	Nut or grape seed oil	50 ml
1/4 cup	Melted butter	50 ml

Part B

1/4 cup	Sundried cranberries	50 ml
1/4 cup	Raisins	50 ml

Mix part A thoroughly, place on baking sheet and bake at 325°F (160°C) for 10 minutes. Stir and then continue to bake until grains turn to a golden brown. Cool and toss with part B.

Serving suggestion: Serve with fresh berries or seasonal fruit.

Dwayne Ennest, Chef
Diner Deluxe

Butternut Squash Pancakes
with Toasted Pecan Syrup

Yields: 6 pancakes

Sift together:

1 1/2 cups	Flour, unbleached all purpose	375 ml
2 tbsp.	Sugar	30 ml
1 1/2 tsp.	Baking powder	7 ml
1 tsp.	Cinnamon, freshly grated	5 ml
1/2 tsp.	Ground ginger	2 ml
1/4 tsp.	Ground cloves	1 ml
1/4 tsp.	Salt	1 ml

Mix together in a second bowl:

1 1/2 cups	Buttermilk	375 ml
1 cup	Butternut squash purée	250 ml
2	Eggs	2
3 tbsp.	Grapeseed oil	45 ml

To make butternut squash purée cut butternut squash in half length ways and roast at 350°F (180°C) till tender, about 40 minutes. Scoop out flesh and purée in food processor. Mix the squash mixture with the flour mixture until there are no lumps. Cook on preheated grill with a little oil until crisp; about 2 minutes per side.

Syrup

1/2 cup	Pecans	125 ml
2 cups	Maple syrup	500 ml

To make the syrup, lightly toast pecans and then finely chop, combine with maple syrup and heat to combine flavours. Serve warm on your favourite pancakes.

Serving suggestion: Serve pancakes immediately with pecan syrup poured on top.

This batter also makes excellent waffles!

Dwayne Ennest, Chef
Diner Deluxe

Crustless Chorizo and Cheddar Quiche

Serves: 4

Preheat oven to 350°F (180°C)

1/2 cup	Flour	125 ml
1 tsp.	Baking powder	5 ml
1/2 tsp.	Dry mustard	2 ml
to taste	Seasoned salt	to taste
2 tbsp.	Parsley, chopped	30 ml
1/2 cup	Milk	125 ml
2–3	Chorizo sausages	2–3
1	Small onion, chopped	1
1 each	Red and yellow pepper, diced	1 each
to taste	Pepper	to taste
8	Eggs	8
1 cup	Milk	250 ml
1/2 cup	White cheddar, grated	125 ml

Combine flour, baking powder, dry mustard, seasoned salt and parsley. Blend with 1/2 cup (125 ml) of milk (add a little more if necessary to make a smooth mixture). Cook chorizo; drain excess grease and slice. Add chopped onion to frying pan and sauté until onions are translucent. Add diced peppers and sauté for 1 minute. Spray a 10 inch (25 cm) pie plate with Pam or an alternate no stick cooking oil spray; cover bottom of plate with chorizo mixture. Meanwhile, add eggs to flour mixture and beat for about a minute, then slowly add 1 cup (250 ml) of milk, mixing thoroughly. Pour this mixture into pie plate and bake for about 35-40 minutes until set. Sprinkle grated cheese over top and return to oven for a minute more, or until the cheese has melted.

Substitutions: If you wish, substitute vegetables or crab for the chorizo — use your imagination, or…clean out your fridge!

Serving suggestions: Serve with a fresh salad for lunch or a toasted bagel for breakfast.

Linda Crossley and Gerrit Visser, Chefs
Village Cantina

Appetizers, Sauces & Sides

Hummus

Serves: 10-12

This delicious chick pea and tahini dip is popular all over the Middle East and is becoming more and more popular everywhere else.

1 lb	Dried chick peas, soaked overnight	500 g
2 tsp.	Baking soda	10 ml
to cover	Water	to cover

Combine chickpeas and baking soda, toss gently and set aside for 10 minutes. Rinse gently, add water, and boil. Reduce heat, allow to simmer, skimming off the foam, until tender; about 2 hours. Rinse a few times and drain well.

6	Garlic cloves	6
1 cup	Tahini paste	250 ml
2 tsp.	Salt	10 ml
2	Lemons, juiced	2
	Parsley for garnish	
	Olive oil for garnish	

Place the garlic in a food processor and mince. Add tahini and enough water to process until creamy. Add 2 cups of chickpeas and process until smooth. Add salt and lemon juice.

Place on a platter and refrigerate until chilled. Can be made ahead by a few days. If there are leftover cooked chickpeas they can be frozen for future use.

Serving suggestions: Serve with pita wedges, raw vegetables or crackers. Garnish with parsley and olive oil.

Aida, Chef
Aida's

Warm Crab Dip

Serves: 8

This wonderful appetizer or party dip can be served either warm or cold.

2 cups	Cream cheese, soft	500 ml
1 cup	Crabmeat, cooked, chopped	250 ml
4 tbsp.	Lemon juice	60 ml
3/4 cup	Parmesan cheese, freshly grated	175 ml
1/2 cup	Artichoke hearts, canned, chopped	125 ml
1 1/2 tsp.	Cayenne pepper	7 ml
to taste	Salt	to taste
to taste	Pepper	to taste

In bowl, mix cream cheese, crabmeat, lemon juice, Parmesan cheese, artichokes and seasoning. Fill ovenproof dish with the mixture to about half an inch from the top. Top with a little fresh Parmesan cheese and bake at 350°F (180°C) for about 15 minutes or until golden brown and bubbling.

Serving suggestions: Cold fresh vegetables, breads, crackers or chips make wonderful dipping accompaniments.

Substitutions: Your favourite shellfish may be used in substitution or in combination with the crab. For example, cooked lobster meat or shrimp. Excellent served with Grey Monk Pinot Gris.

John Skinner, Executive Chef
Cannery Row

Cannery Row's Crab Cakes

Yields: 10 cakes

1 lb	Crabmeat, canned **or** fresh, shredded	500 g
2	Eggs	2
1/3 cup	Dijon mustard	75 ml
1 tsp.	Chipotle peppers finely chopped **or** dried chili flakes	5 ml
1 1/2 tsp.	Worcestershire sauce	7 ml
1/2 cup	Onions; red, white and green minced and mixed	125 ml
1 1/4 cup	Bread crumbs, fine	300 ml
pinch each	Salt and pepper	pinch each

In a large bowl mix all ingredients with your hands until well combined. Form and press 2–3 oz. (55-85 g) patties, about 3/4 inch (2 cm) thick. If the mixture is crumbly when formed into cakes add another half an egg. If mixture is too moist add a small amount of breadcrumbs and mix thoroughly. At this point your crab cakes can be frozen for later use or used right away.

To cook, heat frying pan over medium-high heat. Fry patties in butter until golden brown on both sides.

Serving suggestions: This is a great appetizer or snack food served with Red Pepper Aioli Sauce (see facing page), and makes a great light lunch when served with a salad. Serve with Sumac Ridge Gewürztraminer from the Okanagan.

John Skinner, Executive Chef
Cannery Row & McQueens Upstairs

Red Pepper Aioli

Yields: 1 1/2 cups (375 ml)

1	Red pepper, small	1
1 cup	Mayonnaise	250 ml
2 tbsp.	Garlic	30 ml
2 tbsp.	Fresh lemon juice	30 ml
1 tsp.	Worcestershire sauce	5 ml
to taste	Salt and pepper	to taste

Roast the red pepper until the skin is dark and crisp. When cool, run under cold water and rub with hand until the crisp skin is removed. Finely chop the flesh. Combine all ingredients in a bowl and adjust seasoning
to taste.

John Skinner, Executive Chef
Cannery Row & McQueens Upstairs

Wild Rice Smoked Scallop Cakes
with Caramelized Shallot and Marmalade

Yields: 18 small cakes

3	Shallots, minced	3
3	Garlic cloves, minced	3
1/2	Red onion, julienned	1/2
1 tbsp.	Cooking oil	15 ml
to taste	Salt and pepper	to taste

Sweat over low-medium heat in 1 tbsp. (15 ml) oil until tender and then let cool.

1 lb	Smoked scallops chopped into small pieces	500 g
2 cups	Wild rice cooked	500 ml
1	Red pepper, minced	1
2 tbsp.	Sesame seeds, toasted	30 ml
2 tbsp.	Oregano	30 ml
2 tbsp.	Chives	30 ml
1 cup	Mayonnaise, home made or good quality	250 ml
2 cups	Breadcrumbs, good quality	500 ml
1 tbsp.	Sesame oil	15 ml
1/2 tsp.	Salt	2 ml
1/2 tsp.	Pepper	2 ml
2 tbsp.	Cooking oil, good quality	30 ml
1 tbsp.	Butter	15 ml

Combine all ingredients except cooking oil and butter and 1/2 cup (125 ml) of bread crumbs, and form into cakes. Freeze long enough to be able to keep firm. Roll in extra breadcrumbs. Pan fry in the cooking oil and butter over medium heat.

Caramelized Shallot and Marmalade

Yields: 2 cups (500 ml)

8	Lemons	8
5 cups	Water	800 ml
1 1/4 cups	Sugar	300 ml
4	Shallots	4
1 tbsp.	Oil	15 ml
1 tbsp.	Sugar	15 ml
1 tbsp.	Chili sauce	15 ml

Zest all of the lemons. Add zest to 2 cups (500 ml) boiling water and cook 5 minutes. Discard water and save lemon zest. Chop all of the lemons and put into 3 cups (750 ml) cold water. Bring this mixture to a boil and simmer for one hour. Strain this mixture, discarding pulp, and save the liquid. Combine the reserved zest, liquid and sugar and boil until jelly consistency is achieved. Let this mixture set overnight. Slice shallots into julienne slices and sauté in 1 tbsp. (15 ml) oil; reduce heat and add sugar and chili sauce, cook until shallots are starting to caramelize slightly. Cool shallots and fold into reserved jelly.

Glen Manzer, Chef
River Café

Digby Scallops
with Cinnamon–Fennel Spiced
Butternut Squash Purée

Serves: 6

Preheat oven to 375°F (190°C)

2 lb	Butternut squash	1 kg
1 tsp.	Fennel seeds	5 ml
1 tsp.	Ground cinnamon	5 ml
6	Large Digby scallops	6
1 cup	Acacia honey	250 ml
3	Shallots, large, julienned	3
6 oz.	Fresh tarragon	170 g
1 cup	Extra virgin olive oil	250 ml
to taste	Salt and pepper, olive oil	to taste

Peel and cut the butternut squash into small pieces of approximately the same size (to allow even roasting), sprinkle with olive oil, salt, pepper and fennel seeds. Bake in oven for at least 45 minutes or until brown and tender to the fork. Transfer the cooked squash into a food processor and purée it with the "pulse" button. Re-season the purée and add the cinnamon to taste. Keep warm.

Dip one side of the scallops in the acacia honey and sear them on that side (without touching) for at least 3 minutes in a very hot non-stick skillet. When properly seared remove scallops and add shallots to the same skillet and caramelize them by adding a little more honey to the pan. In a blender gently purée tarragon with olive oil and then strain it through a fine mesh sieve.

Serving suggestion and assembly of dish: Put one dollop of squash purée in the centre of a large dinner plate. Place scallop on top with the caramelized shallots and drizzle the tarragon oil around the plate as a flavourful garnish.

Giuseppe di Gennaro, Chef
Il Sogno

Grilled Oysters
with Spicy Lime Condiment, Fried Garlic and Red Pepper Concasser

Yields: 12

12	Shucked oysters	12
1	Lime, juiced	1
1 tsp.	Tabasco sauce	5 ml
2 tbsp.	Chopped Italian parsley	30 ml
1	Garlic clove, peeled, chopped very thinly and fried	1
1	Red pepper (cleaned of seeds and pith) diced very small	1
1 tbsp.	Thai fish sauce	15 ml

Assembly of dish: Top oysters with a pinch of each ingredient and place under a pre-heated salamander or a home broiler for at least 45 seconds.

Serving suggestion: Serve nicely arranged on a platter.

Giuseppe di Gennaro, Chef
Il Sogno

Pacific Salmon on Dome
with Lollo Rosso on Lobster Infused Sour Cream

Serves: 4

Tequila Cured Salmon

3 lb	Spring salmon filet, skin on, scaled and de-boned	1.5 kg
1 lb	Coarse sea salt or kosher salt	500 g
2 lb	Sugar	1 kg
1 tbsp.	White pepper, ground	15 ml
12	Juniper berries	12
3	Bay leaves	3
3 oz.	Fresh dill	80 ml
1 each	Organic orange and lemon, sliced	1 each
2 oz.	Tequila	55 ml

Place salmon filet in glass casserole. Blend salt, sugar and pepper. Put herbs, spices, citrus and tequila on salmon filet and top it with salt mixture. Cover with plastic wrap. Place a small tray on top of salmon and put up to a 4 lb (2 kg) weight on top. Cure in fridge for 24–36 hours. Scrape off salt and citrus with the back of a kitchen knife. Slice thinly 1/8 inch (3 mm) thick and set aside in fridge for later use.

Salmon Tartar

10 oz.	Salmon filet, cleaned, no skin, no bones, diced to 3/16 inch (2mm)	300 g
2	Shallots, small, finely diced	2
1 tbsp.	Capers, chopped	15 ml
2	Fresh dill stems, coarsely chopped	2
8	Chives, finely sliced	8
1 tbsp.	Olive oil, extra virgin	15 ml
1 or to taste	Lemon, juiced	1 or to taste
to taste	Sea salt	to taste
to taste	Fresh ground white pepper	to taste

Mix all above ingredients together and season to taste.

Assembly of Timbale

Brush four espresso cups or small ramekins with extra virgin olive oil and line inside with Tequila cured salmon slices; have pieces overlapping rim. Fill cups with salmon tartar firmly and close them with overlapping cured salmon. Rest for 15 minutes in fridge.

Garnish

1 oz.	Salmon caviar	30 g
1 tbsp.	Lobster reduction	15 ml
14 oz.	Sour cream	400 g
2 heads	Baby Lollo Rosso, washed	2 heads

Rip off the red tips of the Lollo Rosso so you get long strings of only the red part. Set aside all ingredients for final assembly.

Smoked Salmon Roses for Garnish

4	Smoked salmon slices	4

Place 4 slices of pre-cut, smoked salmon on a cutting board and cut off 1/2 inch (1 cm) strip from the long side (skin side) to make four ribbons of salmon. Roll the remaining salmon into four rolls. Tie the bottom of the roll securely with the ribbon of salmon to create a base to stand on. Stand them up and open the top of each roll so it looks like a rose. The rolls should be 2 inches (5 cm) tall.

Assembly of dish: Make a 4–5 inch (10–13 cm) circle of sour cream in the middle of four plates. Slap plate bottom to smooth. Ring with Lollo Rosso. Gently remove Salmon Timbale from cups and place in the middle of the sour cream. Every inch (2.5 cm) place a dot of lobster reduction in the sour cream. With the tip of a knife, draw through each dot, creating a heart. Place 3-5 caviar eggs in between hearts. Place Salmon Rose on top of Timbale. Place two 4-inch (10 cm) chives inside the rose.

Martin Heusser, Executive Chef
Owl's Nest

Wildwood Mussels

Serves: 1

3 tbsp.	Olive oil	45 ml
1 tbsp.	Red onion, sliced	15 ml
2 tbsp.	Leeks julienned	30 ml
2 tbsp.	Fresh tomato diced	30 ml
1 1/2 tbsp.	Sundried tomato	22 ml
3–5	Fresh garlic cloves, roasted	3–5
to taste	Chipotle pepper chopped	to taste
12 oz.	Fresh mussels	375 g
1 1/2 oz.	White wine	45 ml
2 oz.	Chicken stock	60 ml
1 1/2 oz.	Tomato sauce	22 ml
2 oz.	Whipping cream	60 ml
1 1/2 tbsp.	Cilantro	22 ml
1 oz.	Asiago cheese	30 g
to taste	Salt and pepper	to taste

In a sauté pan, heat the olive oil to a medium heat and add onion, leeks, tomato, sundried tomato, garlic and chipotle pepper. Sauté for 1 minute on high heat, add mussels, and sauté for 1 more minute. Flash with wine, add all other liquids, season with salt and pepper, stir once then cover with a lid and cook for about 2–4 minutes or until the mussels open. Once the mussels are open, place the mussels only in a bowl. Add cilantro and the Asiago to the sauce and stir. If the sauce is too thick, add a touch more stock or wine, then pour over the mussels.

Serving suggestion: A wine recommended by Wildwood is Pepperwood Grove Viognier, California.

Josef Wiewer, Executive Chef
Wildwood

Warm Artichoke Dip
with Fresh Salsa

Serves: 4

4 oz.	Cream cheese	125 g
1/4 cup	Sour cream	250 ml
2 tbsp.	Mayonnaise	30 ml
1 tsp.	Fresh lemon juice	5 ml
8 rings	Pickled hot pepper rings	8 rings
4	Marinated artichoke hearts	4
2	10 inch (25 cm) salsa tortillas	2
1 tbsp.	Fresh Salsa	15 ml

Combine cream cheese, sour cream, mayonnaise and lemon juice in food processor. Chop pickled hot pepper rings and artichoke hearts. Add to cream cheese mixture and pulse until just mixed. Pour into ovenproof dish and bake approximately 10 minutes until bubbling. Cut tortillas into triangles and spread on baking sheet. Bake for about 5 minutes, just until crispy. Serve dip with fresh salsa. Arrange tortilla triangles around dip on a large platter.

Fresh Salsa
Yields: 1–2 cups

1 or 2	Ripe tomatoes	1 or 2
1	Sweet onion	1
1 each	Sweet red and yellow peppers	1 each
2 tbsp.	Fresh cilantro, chopped	30 ml
1	Fresh lime, squeezed	1
to taste	Pickled hot pepper rings	to taste
to taste	Salt	to taste

Dice tomatoes, onion, sweet peppers and pickled hot peppers (I like a fairly fine dice so I can load up my chips). Add cilantro, juice of fresh lime and salt. Depending on the heat you like in your salsa, increase pickled hot peppers, or add fresh minced jalapeno peppers.

Linda Crossley and Gerrit Visser, Chefs
Village Cantina

Spanikopizza

*Yields: 1 large triangle which can be cut
into any number of smaller triangles.*

5	Phyllo pastry sheets	5
3 tbsp.	Pesto sauce	4 5 ml
3 tbsp.	Sundried tomatoes, packed in oil, drained	45 ml
1/2 cup	Spinach, chopped, cooked, drained, packed	125 ml
4 tbsp.	Feta cheese crumbled	60 ml
	Olive oil for brushing	

Brush first sheet of phyllo pastry with olive oil and fold according to diagram. Brush next sheet of phyllo and place first triangle on top of second sheet on section B, upside down, and fold again. Each time, rotate the triangle to make sure a fold seals all sides. Repeat until all sheets are used. Spread finished triangle with pesto sauce. Sprinkle with sundried tomatoes, spinach and Feta cheese.

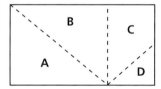

Fold A over B and C over A, and then tuck D under the newly formed triangle. Rotate by placing the first triangle on top of section B and then repeat the folding order until all sheets are used.

Bake for 5-10 minutes or until crisp and golden brown at 350°F (180°C)

Serving suggestions: Cut finished triangle into smaller triangles. Can be made ahead of time and baked from frozen.

Linda Crossley and Gerrit Visser, Chef
Village Cantina

Peppercorn Chicken Wrap

Serves: 4

4 oz.	Cream cheese	125 g
1/4 cup	Sour cream	250 ml
2 tbsp.	Mayonnaise	30 ml
1 tsp.	Fresh lemon juice	5 ml
8 rings	Pickled hot pepper rings	8 rings
4	Marinated artichoke hearts	4
2	10 inch (25 cm) salsa tortillas	2
1 tbsp.	Fresh Salsa	15 ml

Combine cream cheese, sour cream, mayonnaise and lemon juice in food processor. Chop pickled hot pepper rings and artichoke hearts. Add to cream cheese mixture and pulse until just mixed. Pour into ovenproof dish and bake approximately 10 minutes until bubbling. Cut tortillas into triangles and spread on baking sheet. Bake for about 5 minutes, just until crispy. Serve dip with fresh salsa. Arrange tortilla triangles around dip on a large platter.

Fresh Salsa

Yields: 1–2 cups

1 or 2	Ripe tomatoes	1 or 2
1	Sweet onion	1
1 each	Sweet red and yellow peppers	1 each
2 tbsp.	Fresh cilantro, chopped	30 ml
1	Fresh lime, squeezed	1
to taste	Pickled hot pepper rings	to taste
to taste	Salt	to taste

Dice tomatoes, onion, sweet peppers and pickled hot peppers (I like a fairly fine dice so I can load up my chips). Add cilantro, juice of fresh lime and salt. Depending on the heat you like in your salsa, increase pickled hot peppers, or add fresh minced jalapeno peppers.

Linda Crossley and Gerrit Visser, Chefs
Village Cantina

Miso-Honey Chilled Prawns

Serves: 20–25

4 lbs.	Shrimp any size, 21–25s preferred	2 kg
2 tbsp.	Lemon juice	30 ml
to taste	Salt	to taste

Shrimp Marinade

2 tbsp.	Olive oil, extra virgin	30 ml
4 tbsp.	Miso paste	60 ml
4 tbsp.	Honey	60 ml
1 tbsp.	Orange juice concentrate	15 ml
4	Garlic cloves, roasted, finely diced	4
2	Shallots, roasted, finely diced	2
1 tbsp.	Sesame seed oil, dark toasted	15 ml
1 tbsp.	Sesame seeds, white and black, toasted	15 ml
1/2 cup	Fresh cilantro, chopped	125 ml
1	Lemon, zest and juice	1

Mix all marinade ingredients together in a bowl.

Peel and de-vein the shrimp, poach in lemon-salted water until cooked. Remove and put in ice water. When cool, remove shrimp and add to marinade. Chill for 1–2 hours before serving.

Serving suggestion: Serve with cocktails before dinner.

Ken Canavan, Executive Chef
Cilantro

BBQ Marinated Portabello Mushroom Steak
with Goat Cheese and Asiago

Serves: 10

Mushroom Marinade

1/4 cup	Red onion, finely chopped	50 ml
3/4 cup	Green onion, finely chopped	175 ml
1 tbsp.	Fresh basil and thyme, chopped	15 ml
1/2 tsp.	Garlic purée	2 ml
2 cups	Balsamic vinegar	500 ml
3/4 cup	Olive oil	400 ml
1 tsp. each	Salt and pepper	5 ml each
10	Portabello mushrooms	10

Remove the stems from the mushrooms, keeping them whole. Combine all the other ingredients to make the marinade. Then pour the marinade over the mushrooms and let sit overnight, turning once.

Cheese Sauce

4 oz.	Asiago cheese	140 g
4 oz.	Goat cheese	140 g
1 cup	33% whipping cream	250 ml
1 tbsp.	Fresh basil and thyme, chopped	5 ml

Reserve approximately half of both cheeses for melting on top of the mushrooms. Melt the remaining ingredients for the cheese sauce in a saucepan on the BBQ at medium heat. Drain the marinade, and grill the mushrooms on the BBQ, turning once. On top of each mushroom add a slice of Asiago and goat cheese, close lid and let melt. Pour the cheese sauce on a plate, place mushrooms on top and sprinkle with fresh chopped basil and thyme. Left over mushrooms can marinate up to seven days.

Serving suggestion: A recommended wine to accompany this dish is 2000, Alsace Willm Pinot Gris.

Ken Canavan, Executive Chef
Cilantro

B'stilla
(Chicken Pie)

Serves: 4–6

Chicken Filling

1	Cornish hen (or a small chicken)	1
1	Large onion, chopped	1
2–3	Garlic cloves, crushed	2–3
2 tbsp.	Fresh cilantro, chopped	30 ml
1 tsp.	Ginger, ground	5 ml
1 tsp.	White pepper	5 ml
pinch	Saffron	pinch
2 tbsp.	Oil	30 ml
1 1/2 cups	Water	375 ml

Sauté onion, garlic, cilantro, ginger, pepper and saffron in oil in a large pot. Add whole Cornish hen or chicken pieces to pot and cook for 5 minutes, turning bird over in spices. Add 1 1/2 cups (375 ml) water, cover and simmer for 45 minutes or until tender.

5	Eggs, lightly beaten	5
1 tbsp.	Icing sugar	15 ml
pinch	Cinnamon	pinch
sprinkle	Orange blossom water	sprinkle

Remove hen from pot and cool. Continue to simmer sauce uncovered, over medium heat until reduced and thickened. Add eggs, sugar, cinnamon and orange blossom water to hot sauce and cook for 2–3 minutes.

Remove chicken meat from bones and add the slivered pieces to the sauce.

Almond Filling

1 cup	Almonds, toasted or blanched, and finely ground	250 ml
to taste	Orange blossom water	to taste
to taste	Icing sugar and cinnamon for garnish	to taste
9–12 sheets	Phyllo pastry	9–12 sheets
	Oil or chicken grease for brushing pan and top	

In small bowl stir together ground almonds, 1-2 tsp. (5–10 ml) icing sugar, sprinkle of cinnamon and a few drops of orange blossom water.

Assembly of dish: To make the B'stilla pie about 1 inch (25mm) thick, take a piece of phyllo pastry and fold the edges under to make a 6 inch (15 cm) circle **(1.)**. Spread chicken filling on circle. Place next phyllo sheet (at least double the size of bottom circle) over the top so you can still fold one side over bottom layer. Before folding over, oil the sheet, then spread almond mixture over circle side. Now fold the phyllo sheet to cover filling. Place one more sheet over pie and tuck edges completely under bottom layer to seal **(2.)**. Repeat procedure to make 3–4 pies.

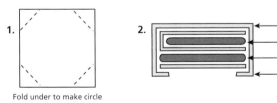

1. Fold under to make circle

2. Top layer / Almond filling / Chicken filling / Tuck under

Brush the B'stilla pies with oil or chicken grease and bake at 375–400°F (190–200°C) for 10–15 minutes. When B'stilla are golden brown, remove from oven, smooth icing sugar over the top and decorate with fine lines of cinnamon.

Ismaili Houssine, Chef
Sultan's Tent

Goat Cheese and Pepper Cheesecake

Serves: 8

1 tbsp.	Olive oil	15 ml
1 cup	Onion, chopped	250 ml
1 tsp.	Garlic, chopped	5 ml
1 tsp.	Shallots, chopped	5 ml
1 cup	Red pepper, chopped	250 ml
2 tsp.	Salt	10 ml
1 tsp.	Pepper	5 ml
1/4 cup	Fresh basil, chopped	50 ml
3–8 oz.	Cream cheese, at room temperature	85–250 g
1 cup	Goat cheese	250 ml
4	Eggs	4

Heat oil, add onion, garlic, shallots, and red pepper and sauté. Add salt, pepper and basil. Remove and let cool. In a mixer, beat together all remaining ingredients and combine with the sautéed vegetables. Pour mixture into a parchment-lined dish 8 x 9 inches (20 x 23 cm). Bake at 300°F (150°C) until very light golden brown.

Serving suggestion: Serve over mixed greens tossed in oil and vinegar.

Michelle Ducie, Associate Chef
Pickled Parrot

Crab Wontons

Yields: 30

Wonton Mix

1 cup	Snow crab	250 ml
1/2 cup	Cream cheese	125 ml
1 tbsp.	Green onion	15 ml
1 tbsp.	Ginger, freshly grated	15 ml
to taste	Ground black pepper	to taste
2 tbsp.	Lemon juice	30 ml
1 pack	Wonton skins (refrigerated section of grocery store)	1 pack
	Vegetable oil for frying	

Combine all ingredients of wonton mix except wonton skins and mix well. Add 1 tsp. (5 ml) of mixture to the center of one wonton skin then bring all 4 corners together to form a tight parcel. Heat oil to 350°F (175°C) in a wok to deep fry the wontons. Fry them for approximately 1 minute or until golden brown and drain on a paper towel.

Sauce

2 cups	Plum sauce	500 ml
2 tbsp	Chili flakes	30 ml
1/2 cup	Fresh cilantro, chopped	125 ml

Mix together plum sauce, chili flakes and cilantro in a bowl.

On a serving plate, pool the sauce so it completely covers the bottom of the plate, arrange wontons on top of the sauce and serve immediately.

Gary Hennessey, Chef
Open Sesame

Kenny's Favourite Tomato Sauce

Yields: 4 cups (1 litre)

4 tbsp.	Quality extra virgin olive oil	60 ml
2	Shallots, thinly sliced	2
6	Garlic cloves, thinly sliced	6
1	Red pepper, finely diced	1
12–15	Green olives, sliced	12–15
10	Ripe tomatoes, diced	10
small bunch	Parsley, coarsely chopped	small bunch
6	Fresh basil leaves, torn	6
1	Juice of large lemon	1
pinch	Chilies, crushed	pinch
to taste	Fresh ground pepper and kosher salt	to taste

Start by sautéing shallots, garlic, red pepper and olives in oil until slightly browned. Add tomatoes and simmer for 10 minutes, stirring regularly. Finish by adding remaining ingredients and season aggressively. Hold for use.

Note: This type of sauce is a mainstay in the restaurant for use on grilled red meats such as veal chops, lamb or beef ribeye and on grilled whitefish such as sea bass, escolar or snapper. It is also an ideal pan braising sauce for fish or poultry. Other ingredients can be added or substituted. Feel free to experiment. Fresh tomatoes are best, but a prepared basic tomato sauce or canned whole tomatoes may be used.

Kenny Kaechele, Chef
The Living Room

Dried Cherry Walnut Bread

Yields: one 8-inch (20 cm) loaf

2 3/4 cups	Flour	675 ml
1 cup	Seven-grain cereal	250 ml
2 tsp.	Baking soda	10 ml
1 tsp.	Baking powder	5 ml
2 cups	Dried cherries	500 ml
2 cups	Walnuts, chopped	500 ml
1/4 cup	Rolled oats	50 ml
1/2 cup	Demerara sugar	125 ml

Mix dry ingredients.

1 cup	Butter, melted	250 ml
3	Eggs	3
1 1/2 cup	Milk	375 ml
1/4 cup	Molasses	50 ml
1/4 cup	Coffee	50 ml
2 tsp.	Vanilla extract	10 ml
1/4 cup	First press Highwood Crossing canola oil	50 ml

Preheat oven to 350°F (180°C). Melt 1 cup (250 ml) of butter. Brush one 8-inch (20 cm) bread pan with 3 tbsp. (45 ml) of the melted butter and dust with flour. Remove excess flour. Add the rest of the wet ingredients to the remaining melted butter. Combine wet and dry ingredients being careful not to over mix. Place in to the prepared pan and bake 40–50 minutes. Let cool 5 minutes, unmould and cool completely.

Glen Manzer, Chef
River Café

Latkes (Potato Pancakes)
with Easy Apple Compote

Yeilds: 16 latkes

Potato Pancakes

2.5 lbs	Russet potatoes, peeled	1.1 kg
1	Fresh lemon, juiced	1
1 tsp.	Fresh parsley, chopped	5 ml
1/2 tsp.	Salt	2 ml
3	Eggs	3
1	Egg yolk	1
1	Medium onion, chopped	1
1/4 tsp.	White pepper, ground	1 ml
1 tsp.	Baking powder	5 ml
4 tbsp.	Flour	60 ml
4 oz.	Canola oil, for frying	125 ml

Grate potatoes, transfer to a sieve and press out as much water as possible. Combine potatoes with fresh squeezed lemon juice first, then add remaining ingredients, except oil. In a large skillet, heat canola oil on medium heat and spoon 2 tbsp. (30 ml) of mixture for each latke and cook 4 minutes per side. Turn carefully with two spatulas so as not to splash hot oil. Drain on paper towel and serve with sour cream and/or Apple Compote.

Apple Compote

6	Granny smith apples, peeled, cored and cut into 1/2 inch (1 cm) dice	6
1 tbsp.	Butter	15 ml
1/2 cup	Sugar	125 ml
1	Fresh lemon, juiced	1
14 oz.	Apple sauce, canned	400 g
14 oz.	Apple pie filling, canned	400 g
1/4 tsp.	Nutmeg	1 ml
1/4 tsp.	Cinnamon	1 ml
1/4 tsp.	Allspice	1 ml

Put apples, butter, sugar and lemon juice into a heavy bottomed sauce pan and cook over medium-low heat for 30 minutes. Add remaining ingredients and simmer covered for 1 hour, stirring occasionally with a wooden spoon.

Note: Apple compote may be refrigerated for up to 7 days or frozen for up to 3 months for later use.

Serving suggestions: You can add 1/2 oz. (15 ml) Apricot Brandy to this recipe and serve with pork roast or chops.

Jim Sarantis, Head Chef
Smuggler's Inn

Roasted Summer Vegetable Terrine
with Yellow Tomato Vinaigrette

Serves: 12

Terrine

2 tbsp.	Fresh basil, chopped	30 ml
1 cup	Olive oil	250 ml
3	Garlic cloves, chopped	3

Combine basil, olive oil, garlic and set aside.

2	Eggplants, sliced lengthwise 1/2 inch thick	2
3	Small zucchini, sliced lengthwise 1/2 inch thick	3
to taste	Salt and pepper	to taste

Brush two sheet pans with olive oil and arrange eggplants and zucchini in a single layer. Brush vegetables with oil mixture and bake at 450°F (230°C) for 10 minutes. Season with salt and pepper, set aside.

7 oz.	Spinach	200 g
pinch	Nutmeg, grated	pinch

Cook spinach in 1 tbsp. (15 ml) of oil mixture, add salt pepper and pinch of nutmeg

4	Red peppers, roasted and peeled	4
7 oz.	Swiss cheese, thinly sliced	200 g

Line terrine mould with plastic wrap and brush with oil. Arrange eggplant on the bottom so they overhang the edge. Next layer zucchini over eggplant. Add layers of roasted pepper, cheese, zucchini and spinach. Alternate vegetables as such until mould is full. Cover by overlapping eggplant. Cook in bain-marie (water bath) for 30 minutes at 400°F (200°C), and let cool.

Vinaigrette

3	Yellow tomatoes, large	3
4 tbsp.	Rice vinegar	60 ml
1 cup	Grape seed oil	250 ml
to taste	Salt and white pepper	to taste

In a blender purée tomatoes with vinegar. Slowly incorporate the oil. Season with salt and pepper. Pass through fine tammi (strainer).

Garnish

Cucumber, finely chopped
Red pepper, finely chopped
Green pepper, finely chopped

To serve, cut terrine in slices, drizzle with vinaigrette and sprinkle with garnish vegetables.

Randy Hollands, Executive Chef
The Ranche Restaurant

Prawns Pousse-Rapière

Serves: 1

Prawns, peeled and deveined 21-25
Olive oil, for frying
Salt and pepper
Armagnac
Oranges, segments for garnish
and some fresh juice

Heat a pan. Quickly sear prawns with a touch of olive oil and salt and pepper to taste. Flambé with Armagnac and then add the orange juice. Place the prawns still slightly undercooked around plate, beside the orange segments. Reduce sauce and pour over top.

Patrice Durandeau, Owner and Dan McKinley, Chef
Fleur de Sel

Sockeye Salmon Cakes
with Chive Crème Fraîche

Serves: 4

Sockeye Salmon Cakes

1 lb.	Fresh sockeye salmon	450 g
	or fresh salmon of your choice	
1/8 cup	Capers, finely minced	25 ml
1/8 cup	Shallots, finely minced	25 ml
2	Large egg whites	2
1 tbsp.	Chili oil*	15 ml
to taste	Salt and pepper	to taste
2 tbsp.	Olive oil	30 ml

With a sharp knife, cut salmon into fine mince. Add the rest of the ingredients and mix well. Shape into eight 2 inch (5 cm) patties and refrigerate for one hour. Heat a nonstick pan and add olive oil. Sauté patties for 1 1/2 minutes on each side and serve warm, two per person.

*To make chili oil, add 1/4 cup (50 ml) crushed chilies to 1 cup (250 ml) canola oil and let sit for 24 hours.

Chive Crème Fraîche

1 cup	Crème fraîche or plain yogurt	250 ml
1 cup	Chives, chopped	250 ml

Blanche chives in boiling, salted water until soft. Plunge in ice water bath. Place chives in blender and purée. Add crème fraîche or yogurt and pulse to blend. Pour through fine mesh strainer. Season with salt and pepper to taste.

Serving suggestion: Place spring mix lettuce (or your favourite variety) in centre of plate. Put 2 salmon cakes on top and drizzle with chive crème fraîche.

Janice Hepburn, Chef
The Living Room

Tropical Fruit Vinaigrette

Yields: 2 cups (500 ml)

1/2 cup	Selected fruit nectar or purée	125 ml
1/2 cup	Champagne vinegar	125 ml
	or white wine vinegar	
1 tsp.	Shallot, minced	5 ml
1 tbsp.	Liquid honey	15 ml
1 1/2 cups	Extra virgin olive oil	375 ml
1 tbsp.	Fresh cilantro, chopped	15 ml
to taste	Kosher salt and white pepper	to taste

In food processor or with hand held mixer, combine all ingredients except olive oil, cilantro, salt and pepper. Add olive oil in slow stream while blending until an emulsion forms. Finish by adding cilantro and stir through. Season to taste and store in refrigerator.

Note: Guava, mango, passion fruit or papaya are all suitable for a fruit purée. These ingredients and many other interesting vinegars are now widely available in better supermarkets and specialty food stores. These vinaigrettes are perfect dressings for any salad greens to accompany lighter entrées or all by themselves.

Kenny Kaechele, Chef
The Living Room

Soups
& Salads

Tabbouli

Serves: 8

Tabbouli is a traditional Lebanese salad, healthy, refreshing and a great accompaniment to any meal.

3 bunches	Parsley, finely chopped	3 bunches
3	Tomatoes, medium, finely chopped	3
9	Green onions, chopped	9
1/4 cup	Fine bulgar wheat, rinsed in cold water and drained	50 ml
1 sm. bunch	Fresh mint, chopped	1 sm. bunch
1/3 tbsp.	**or** dried mint	5 ml
1 cup	Olive oil	250 ml
1 tsp.	Salt	5 ml
1 tsp.	Black pepper	5 ml
3	Fresh lemons, juiced	3

Combine all ingredients in a mixing bowl.

Serving suggestions: Serve with your favourite meal.

Aida, Chef
Aida's

Chilled Summer Gazpacho Soup

Serves: 4

A delightfully refreshing and easy to make summertime soup, that only gets better with age. This soup can be left thick and hearty or puréed into smooth soup.

1 cup	Tomato, peeled and de-seeded, small dice	250 ml
1/2 cup	Celery, small dice	125 ml
1/2 cup	Cucumber, peeled and de-seeded, small dice	125 ml
1/2 cup	Green pepper, small dice	125 ml
1/3 cup	Green onion or onion, small dice	75 ml
2 tbsp.	Parsley, chopped	30 ml
1 clove	Garlic, minced	1 clove
2 1/2 cups	Tomato juice (V8 juice if desired)	625 ml
2 tbsp.	Olive oil	30 ml
3 tbsp.	White wine vinegar	45 ml
1 tsp.	Worcestershire sauce	5 ml
to taste	Salt and pepper	to taste

In a large bowl or pot, mix the tomatoes, celery, cucumber, green pepper, onion, parsley and garlic. Then add the tomato juice, olive oil, wine vinegar and Worcestershire sauce. Mix until combined and refrigerate for a minimum of four hours or even better, overnight. Season with salt and pepper to taste and enjoy.

Serving suggestions: Sprinkle a few fresh basil croutons on top for garnish if you wish. Fresh baked bread is a great accompaniment. Sprinkle cooked baby shrimp on top for a variation and accompany with a bottle of Red Rooster Riesling, Okanagan.

John Skinner, Executive Chef
Cannery Row & McQueens Upstairs

Winter Squash Soup
with Chutney and Vanilla Oil

Serves: 12

4 lbs.	Winter squash	2 kg
to taste	Salt and pepper, oil	to taste
1 cup	White wine	250 ml
6	Garlic cloves, minced	6
3 tbsp.	Fresh ginger, minced	45 ml
1 cup	Shallots, minced	250 ml
1 cup	Carrots, 1/4 inch (0.5 cm) dice	250 ml
1 cup	Leeks, white part only, washed and chopped	250 ml
3 cups	Yellow onion, 1/4 inch (0.5 cm) dice	750 ml
1 cup	Celery, 1/4 inch (0.5 cm) dice	250 ml
1 cup	Parsnip, 1/4 inch (0.5 cm) dice	250 ml
5 cups	Vegetable stock	1.2 litres
2 cups	Apple cider	500 ml
1/2 cup	Orange juice concentrate	125 ml
1/2 cup	Maple syrup	125 ml
1	Cinnamon sticks	1
1/2 tsp.	Nutmeg, grated	2 ml
1/2 tsp.	Cinnamon, ground	2 ml
1/2 tsp.	Ground ginger	2 ml
14 oz.	Coconut milk, canned	400 ml

Preheat the oven to 375°F (190°C). Cut squash in half and remove any seeds. Season the squash with salt and pepper. Lightly oil a baking pan and place the squash, cut side down, on the pan. Pour wine over squash and bake for approximately 45 minutes, or until tender. Let cool completely. Scrape flesh out of squash and set aside.

In a heavy stockpot, heat oil over medium heat. Add garlic, ginger, shallots, carrots, leeks, onion, celery and parsnip and a sprinkling of salt. Reduce heat and sauté with no colour for 25–35 minutes. Mix in the cooked squash, stock, cider, orange juice concentrate, maple syrup, spices and coconut milk. Simmer for 20 minutes. Let cool and purée in a blender (in batches) until smooth. Press through a fine-meshed sieve. Heat the soup and add more stock if it's too thick.

To serve, ladle into soup bowls and garnish with Chutney and Vanilla Oil.

Vanilla Oil

Yields: 3 cups (750 ml)

3 cups	Grapeseed oil	750 ml
2	Star anise	2
3	Bay leaves	3
2	Cinnamon sticks	2
2 tbsp.	Vanilla extract	30 ml
6	Vanilla beans	6

In non-reactive pot combine grapeseed oil, star anise, bay leaves, cinnamon sticks and vanilla extract. Split and scrape vanilla beans into mixture. Over very low heat, cook out vanilla extract until just oil remains, no liquid. Let cool and store in airtight container in refrigerator.

(Continued on following page)

Winter Squash Soup
with Chutney and Vanilla Oil
(continued)

Spiced Current Chutney

Yields: 3 cups (750 ml)

1 tbsp.	Cooking oil	15 ml
1 cup	Shallots, julienne	250 ml
1 tbsp.	Fresh garlic, minced	15 ml
3 tbsp.	Fresh ginger, minced	45 ml
1/4 cup	Demerara sugar	50 ml
1/2 cup	Cider vinegar	125 ml
1 cup	Vegetable stock	250 ml
3 tbsp.	Port	45 ml
2 tbsp.	Brandy	30 ml
1 tsp.	Ground juniper	5 ml
1 tsp.	Chipotle pepper, minced	5 ml
1/4 tsp.	Nutmeg, ground	1 ml
1/4 tsp.	Cinnamon, ground	1 ml
1/4 tsp.	Ginger, ground	1 ml
1	Whole cinnamon stick	1
10 oz.	Dried currants	375 g
1/2 tsp.	Salt and pepper	2 ml
3 tbsp.	Fresh parsley, chopped	45 ml
1 tbsp.	Fresh sage, chopped	15 ml

In 1 tbsp. (15 ml) of oil, sauté prepared shallots, garlic and ginger for 3 minutes. Add remaining ingredients except for fresh herbs and cook until all liquid is reduced completely. Let cool completely and stir in reserved chopped herbs.

Glen Manzer, Chef
River Café

Dandelion Greens Vinaigrette

Yields: 4 1/2 cups (1 litre)

4 oz.	Dandelion greens, chopped	125 g
1/8 cup	Shallot, minced	25 ml
1/2 tbsp.	Grain mustard	7.5 ml
1 oz.	Garlic flower	30 g
1 cup	Basil oil	250 ml
1/4 tsp.	Black pepper, ground	1 ml
1/2 tsp.	Salt	2 ml
3/4 cup	Grapeseed oil	187 ml
1 cup	Olive oil	250 ml
3/4 cup	Unflavoured rice vinegar	187 ml
1 oz.	Maple syrup	30 g
1/8 tsp.	Chipotle pepper in adobo	0.5 ml

Combine all prepared ingredients in a non-reactive bowl, mixing thoroughly. Purée vinaigrette in batches in a food processor until the vinaigrette is finished. Store in airtight container in refrigerator.

Serving suggestions: This vinaigrette is fantastic on fish — preferably salmon or halibut with a nice ripe tomato salad. Sauvignon Blanc is an appropriate accompanying wine.

Glen Manzer, Chef
River Café

Tom Yum Soup
(Shrimp Soup)

Serves: 3–4

3 cups	Shrimp and/or chicken stock	750 ml
6–8	White mushrooms, halved	6–8
1 or to taste	Fresh Thai chili*, thinly sliced	1 or to taste
1	Lemon grass stalk	1
7 slices	Galanga*	7 slices
4–5	Kaffir lime leaves	4–5
1 tsp.	Salt	5 ml
1 tbsp.	Fish sauce (omit salt if using fish sauce)	15 ml
1 tbsp.	Fresh lime juice	15 ml
12	Tiger shrimp, fresh or frozen	12

Prepare all ingredients before starting, as cooking time is about 8 minutes. To prepare lemon grass, peel off outer layers and use the bottom 8 inch (20 cm) of the stalk. Slice on the diagonal, 1/8 inch (2 mm) thick. Shell and devein shrimp, reserve shells for stock. Slice galanga 1/8 inch (2 mm) thick. Bring stock to a boil in a medium saucepan. You may reserve the shells from the shrimp and boil for 5 minutes in 2 cups of water and add 1 cup of chicken stock or, use only chicken stock. Once stock is boiling add mushrooms first. Add all other ingredients, adding shrimp last. Cook for 2 minutes at a rolling boil. Be careful not to over cook the shrimp. If you are using chicken, add the chicken to the boiling broth first, then mushrooms and then the other ingredients. Cook chicken for at least 6 minutes.

Serving suggestions: Serve in a large serving bowl. Garnish with chopped green onion, chopped fresh cilantro and minced fresh chilies (optional for a hotter dish).

Substitutes: Thinly sliced chicken breast can be substituted for the shrimp.

Chef's Vanh, Sonthaya, Vida and Kalayarat
Thai-Sa-On

Cream of Traditional Ale

Serves: 4

1/3 cup	Butter	75 ml
1	Small onion, chopped	1
1 cup	Leek, chopped	250 ml
1	Celery stalk, chopped	1
1	Medium carrot, chopped	1
2 cups	Chicken broth	500 ml
1 bottle	Traditional Ale (or Brown Ale)	1 bottle
2	Medium potatoes, peeled and cubed	2
to taste	Salt	to taste
to taste	Pepper	to taste
to taste	Oregano	to taste
1 cup	Cereal cream	250 ml
	Parsley, fresh and chopped for garnish	

Heat butter in a large saucepan over medium–high heat. Add chopped vegetables and sauté for 2 minutes. Pour in chicken stock and beer, add potatoes, salt, pepper and oregano. Bring to a boil. Reduce heat and simmer for 30 minutes.

Pour soup into a food processor and purée until smooth. Place soup back into sauce pan, add cereal cream and adjust seasoning. Sprinkle with chopped parsley.

Serving suggestion: Serve with whole wheat baguette.

Klaus Wöckinger, Chef/Owner
Big Rock Grill

Warm Balsamic Root Vegetable Salad

Serves: 1

Marinade for Feta Cheese

3 tbsp.	Olive oil	40 ml
1	Garlic clove	1
1	Fresh oregano twig	1
2	Basil leaves	2
1	Lemon, juiced	1
3 oz.	Feta cheese	85 g

Mix together all ingredients and pour over feta cheese. Marinate overnight.

Root Vegetables and Dressing

1 oz.	Turnip	30 g
1 oz.	Rutabaga	30 g
1 oz.	Parsnip	30 g
1 oz.	Carrot	30 g
1 oz.	Beet	30 g

Cut all vegetables into batonnet shapes 2 x 3/8 inch (5 x 0.5 cm). Blanch separately to "al dente" in boiling, salted water. Begin with the white vegetable and finish with the darkest (beet). Chill vegetables in ice water. Set aside.

Dressing

1/4 tsp.	Caraway	1 g
1	Garlic clove, crushed	1
2 tbsp.	Olive oil, extra virgin	30 ml
1	Winteris turkey chorizo sausage, sliced	1
2 tbsp.	White balsamic vinegar	30 ml
to taste	Sea salt, sugar, black pepper	to taste

Sauté caraway and garlic in olive oil; add the Winteris Turkey slices and blanched root vegetables. After 3-4 minutes glaze with balsamic vinegar. Season to taste with sea salt, sugar and fresh-ground black pepper from the mill.

Vinaigrette for Salad

2 tbsp.	Aged balsamic	30 ml
to taste	Salt, sugar, pepper	to taste
1	Shallot, diced	1
1 tsp.	Dijon mustard	5 ml
5 tbsp.	Olive oil, extra virgin	60 ml
2 oz.	Mesclun greens	55 g

Mix all ingredients except oil and greens in a bowl. Add the oil and blend with a whisk. Toss with mesclun.

Garnish

1	Scallion, sliced thinly	1
1	Carrot swirls	1

Assembly of dish: Place feta cheese on one side of oval plate and arrange warm vegetables with dressing beside. Garnish with scallion rings or carrot swirls. Make a nice bouquet with mesclun greens on the opposite side. Enjoy!

Martin Heusser, Executive Chef
Owl's Nest

Som Tum
(Papaya and Carrot Salad)

Serves: 2

1 cup	Papaya, pounded or shredded	250 ml
1 cup	Carrots, shredded or cut into fine julienned strips	250 ml
2	Fresh garlic cloves, chopped (optional)	2
1 or 2	Fresh chilies, sliced (to taste) (You may substitute 1 tsp. (5 ml) of dried chilies, but do not add to the mixture until the end)	1 or 2
1 tsp.	Salt (or to taste)	5 ml
1 tbsp.	Fish sauce (if using Fish Sauce, omit the salt)	15 ml
1 tbsp.	Fresh lime juice	15 ml
1/2	Tomato, sliced	1/2

Garnish

2 tbsp.	Peanuts, ground, unsalted **or** chopped cashew nuts	30 ml
to taste	Dried shrimp	to taste

Start by mixing the papaya, carrots, garlic, and fresh chilies. Do not use an electric mixer or food processor! Ideally use a mortar and pestle. Otherwise mix aggressively in a stainless steel mixing bowl or pulverize between a knife handle and a strong breadboard. However you do it, ingredients should be mixed and pounded thoroughly. After a few minutes of mixing, add fish sauce or salt, sugar, tomatoes and lime juice. Pound again, turning mixture over repeatedly until you arrive at an even texture and everything is well blended.

Serving suggestions: Serve on a serving dish at the table with garnish. Blue and white are the traditional colours of serving dishes in Thailand.

Chef's Vanh, Sonthaya, Vida and Kalayarat
Thai-Sa-On

Tom-Kha-Kai Soup
(Chicken Soup)

Serves: 5–6

Chicken in spicy coconut milk with galanga and lemon grass. This soup is found on the menu of virtually every Thai restaurant in Siam.

8 oz.	Chicken tenderloin, cut into bite-size pieces **or** use chicken breast	250 g
5 cups	Chicken broth	1.15 litres
1	Lemon grass stalk, cut into pieces	1
4	Dried galanga slices	4
2	Kafir lime leaves	2
4 tsp.	Nam Pla (fish sauce)	20 ml
2	Fresh chilies, cut into small pieces	2
2	Green onions, cut into small pieces	2
14 oz.	Coconut milk, canned (thick)	400 ml
1 tsp.	Lime juice	5 ml
	Coriander leaves for garnish	

In a saucepan, combine and simmer the chicken, chicken broth, lemon grass, kaffir lime leaves, fish sauce, chili and green onions. Cook for about 10 minutes, making sure the chicken is cooked but do not over cook. Just before serving, add thick coconut milk, lime juice and more fish sauce if needed (taste first). Note: Use more coconut milk to thicken soup if necessary.

Garnish with fresh coriander.

Bingo Chung and Helen Chung, Executive Chefs
The King and I

A-Jaad
(Cucumber Salad)

Serves: 4

1/2 cup	Vinegar	125 ml
2 tbsp.	Sugar	30 ml
1 tsp.	Salt	5 ml
2 tbsp.	Cut red chilies	30 ml
1/2 cup	Shallots, sliced	125 ml
1 cup	Cucumber, sliced	250 ml
	Coriander leaves for garnish	

Melt sugar and salt in the vinegar, and then add the cut chilies, sliced shallots and cucumber. Chill.

Serving suggestions: Spread cucumbers on a platter or in a bowl and garnish with some coriander leaves for decoration and flavour.

Bingo Chung and Helen Chung, Executive Chefs
The King and I

Butternut Squash and Pancetta Soup

Serves: 10–15

3	Butternut squash, large	3
1/2 cup	Pancetta (Italian bacon), diced small	125 ml
1 cup	Red onion, small, diced	250 ml
1 tsp.	Fresh garlic, minced	5 ml
1 tsp.	Shallots, minced	5 ml
1/2 cup	White wine	125 ml
10 cups	Water	2.5 litres
1/4 cup	Fresh basil, chopped	50 ml
2 cups	Cream	500 ml
to taste	Salt and pepper	to taste

Cut squash in half and roast at 375°F (190°C) inside down, until it becomes quite soft. Let cool. As squash is roasting dice the pancetta and fry in large soup pot on medium heat. You want the fat to cook out. Slowly add the diced red onion along with the garlic and shallots. (Don't let the garlic get too dark, you want it to cook not burn.) When the onion and garlic are a very light golden brown deglaze with white wine. Slowly add 10 cups (2.5 L) of water and the chopped basil. Simmer for 15 minutes. When squash has cooled separate the inside from the skin, put in a bowl and mash. Whisk the squash purée into the liquid, add cream and simmer for 15 minutes. Then add salt and pepper to taste.

Serving suggestion: Serve with fresh, crusty bread.

Michelle Ducie, Associate Chef
Pickled Parrot

Pork Cheek Confit Salad
with Mixed Greens and
Roasted Tomato Vinaigrette

Serves: 8

10 oz.	Pork cheeks, trimmed of all excess fat and glands	300 g
2 tbsp.	Coarse salt	30 ml
2 tbsp.	Fresh thyme leaves	30 ml
1 tsp.	Black peppercorns, whole	5 ml
1 2/3 cups	Duck fat	400 ml
1 2/3 cups	Pork fat	400 ml

Season the pork cheeks with all of the salt, thyme and black peppercorns. Place on perforated insert or rack with a deep insert or dish underneath to catch any dripping blood. Cover and refrigerate for 12 hours. Remove from the fridge and wipe off excess salt. Mix the two fats together and heat to 175°F (100°C), in a Pyrex dish, in the oven. Place the cheeks in the fat and cook for 1 1/2 hours. If they start to colour reduce heat. Sterilize a clean jar or container with a lid. Using sterile tongs gently remove the meat and place in the jar. Pour the fat over top to completely cover the cheeks. Cover and let cool for two hours before putting in refrigerator. Let it age for 2–3 weeks in the refrigerator.

To serve, slowly heat until fat is melted. Carefully remove cheeks. Slice thinly 1/8 inch (3 mm) against the grain and lay flat on a baking sheet. Heat in a hot oven to crisp.

Serving suggestions: Dress salad greens with roasted tomato vinaigrette (see facing page) and garnish salad with crispy cheeks.

Roasted Tomato Vinaigrette

Serves: 8

6	Roma tomatoes cut into half	6
1 tbsp.	Sugar	15 ml
4 tbsp.	Balsamic vinegar	50 ml
1 cup	Canola oil	100 ml
4 tbsp.	Grapeseed oil	50 ml
1 tsp.	Salt	5 ml

Roast the tomatoes in the oven for about 15 minutes at 350°F (180°C). Purée the roasted tomatoes with the sugar in a food processor. With the motor running, slowly add the vinegar. Slowly add the oils and salt. Pass through a sieve to remove the skins and seeds.

Michael Allemeier
Teatro

Chilled Citrus Soup

Serves: 4

2 cups	Mango purée, about 3 mangoes	500 ml
4 tbsp.	Sugar syrup, see below	60 ml
1 cup	Gewürztraminer wine	250 ml
1/2 cup	Fresh orange juice	100 ml
1	Lemon, juiced	1

Purée mangos, add the rest of the ingredients and chill. This can be prepared up to a day in advance. Serve in small glasses.

Sugar Syrup

| 1/2 cup | Water | 100 ml |
| 5 tbsp. | White sugar | 80 g |

Bring water and sugar to a boil. Remove from heat source and let cool.

Serving suggestion: A nice added touch is to place a small scoop of sorbet on top of soup just before serving. Any leftover sugar syrup can be used anywhere you can use liquid sugar, such as in coffee or tea.

Suzanne Taylor, Pastry Chef
Delta Bow Valley

Citrus Caesar Delight

Serves: 8

1	Garlic clove, minced	1
1/2 cup	Vegetable oil	125 ml
1 tsp.	Granulated sugar	5 ml
to taste	Salt	to taste
1/2 tsp.	Worcestershire sauce	2 ml
1/4 tsp.	Dry mustard	1 ml
1/4 tsp.	Paprika	1 ml
4 tsp.	Rice wine vinegar	20 ml
4 tsp.	Lemon juice	20 ml
8 cups	Romaine lettuce, torn	2 litres
1 cup	Mandarin oranges, slices	250 ml
	Croutons and Parmesan cheese, for garnish	

In a bowl, combine garlic, oil, sugar, salt, Worcestershire sauce, mustard and paprika. Mix thoroughly and refrigerate overnight. Prior to serving, add vinegar and lemon juice and stir well. Mix together romaine lettuce with mandarin oranges. Pour on dressing and toss lightly. Garnish with croutons and Parmesan cheese.

Jake Kirchner, Executive Chef
Carver's Steakhouse

Corn Chowder
with Cilantro Oil and Red Pepper Coulis

Serves: 8

4 oz.	Onion, medium dice	100 g
3 1/2 oz.	Carrot, medium dice	75 g
3 1/2 oz.	Celery, medium dice	75 g
3 1/2 oz.	Butter	75 g
3 1/2 oz.	Flour	75 g

Heat the butter in a heavy sauce pot. Add the onion, carrot and celery and cook but do not brown. Now add the flour and stir to a roux. Cook roux for 4–5 minutes, but do not brown.

4 cups	Chicken stock	1 litre
1 cup	Cream corn	250 ml
14 oz.	Frozen corn kernels	400 g
14 oz.	Potatoes, medium dice	400 g

Using a wire whisk, slowly stir in the stock and cream corn. Bring to a boil, stirring to make sure liquid is smooth. Add the potatoes and corn kernels. Simmer until vegetables are tender.

1 cup	Milk, hot	250 ml
1/2 cup	Heavy cream, hot	100 ml
to taste	Salt and white pepper	to taste

Stir in hot milk and cream, season to taste with salt and white pepper.

Red Pepper Coulis

1	Red pepper	1
to taste	Salt and white pepper	to taste

Roast the red pepper, peel, de-seed, then blend and strain. Season to taste.

Cilantro Oil

1/2 bunch	Cilantro, leaves only	1/2 bunch
1 cup	Canola oil	250 ml
to taste	Salt and white pepper	to taste

Mix cilantro and canola oil in a blender and season to taste.

Note: Red pepper coulis and cilantro oil can be prepared well in advance.

Presentation notes: Fill soup bowl 3/4 full. Swirl the cilantro oil and red pepper coulis on top.

C.R. (Bob) Matthews, Executive Chef
La Chaumière Restaurant

Grilled Romaine Salad

Serves: 1

1/2	Romaine lettuce heart, halved	1/2
1/2 oz.	Vegetable oil	15 ml
pinch	Coarse salt and white pepper	pinch
2 oz.	Tomato vinaigrette	60 ml
1 oz.	Caesar dressing	30 ml
1	Goat cheese fritter	1
1	Roma tomatoes, roasted	1
5	Garlic cloves, roasted	5
1 oz.	Red onions, julienned and fried	30 ml
	Parsley for garnish	

Toss romaine hearts in oil, season well with salt and white pepper. Place on grill for 5 minutes until well grilled. Spread tomato vinaigrette on the bottom of a large oval plate. Put romaine hearts crossed on top of tomato vinaigrette. From a squeeze bottle, drizzle Caesar dressing across both romaine hearts. Place goat cheese fritter on top of hearts and roasted tomato on the side of fritter. Sprinkle the garlic cloves around plate. Spread fried onions on top of fritter and tomato. Finish with some parsley.

Alternative for goat cheese fritters: Sprinkle crumbled goat cheese over whole salad.

Steve Little, Executive Chef
4th Street Rose

Soongs
(Lettuce Cups)

Yields: 5–6 cups

4 oz.	Chicken breast, finely diced	115 g
1 oz.	Onion, finely diced	30 g
1 oz.	Water chestnuts (canned), finely diced	30 g
1 oz.	Mushrooms, finely diced	30 g
1 tsp.	Ginger, freshly grated	5 ml
1 tsp.	Garlic, crushed	5 ml
2 tbsp.	Canola oil	30 ml
2 tbsp.	Soy sauce	30 ml
1 tsp.	Sugar	5 ml
6 tbsp.	Hoisin sauce	90 ml
1 tsp.	Sesame oil	5 ml
1 head	Iceberg lettuce	1 head

Combine chicken, onion, water chestnuts, mushrooms, ginger and garlic in a bowl. Heat canola oil in wok, add chicken mixture and stir constantly for 30 seconds. Then add soy sauce, sugar, 2 tbsp. (30 ml) Hoisin sauce and sesame oil and cook through for 2 minutes stirring constantly. Transfer to serving bowl.

Cut lettuce in half, lengthways and remove inner layers, leaving 5 or 6 good layers.

To serve, spoon chicken mixture into a lettuce cup and roll into a parcel. Using your fingers, dip into Hoisin sauce.

Serving suggestion: Serve on a nacho-style plate with separate compartments and add Hoisin sauce in the centre.

Gary Hennessy, Chef
Open Sesame

Sultan's Tent Harira Soup
(Tomato and Lentil Soup)

Serves 10

Harira soup traditionally breaks Ramadan fast.

10 cups	Water	2.5 litres
2 cups	Large onions, coarsely chopped	500 ml
1 cup	Cilantro, chopped and blended	250 ml
1 cup	Parsley, chopped and blended	250 ml
1 cup	Celery, chopped and blended	250 ml
1 tsp.	White pepper	5 ml
1 tbsp.	Ginger, ground	15 ml
1 tbsp.	Paprika	15 ml
2 tsp.	Salt	10 ml
1 tbsp.	Oil	15 ml
1/8 tsp.	Saffron, ground	1 ml
44 oz.	Canned tomatoes with juice	1.3 litres
2 cups	Green lentils, soaked in hot water for 15 minutes	500 ml
2 cups	**or** cooked chickpeas	500 ml
1 cup	Rice or small pasta like orzo	250 ml
1/2 cup	Flour	125 ml

Heat 6 cups (1.5 litres) of water in a large soup pot. Place onions, cilantro, parsley and celery in a blender or food processor, add 1–2 cups (250–500 ml) more water and blend until smooth. Add to pot. Stir in white pepper, ginger, paprika, salt, oil and saffron. Simmer soup for 10–15 minutes.

Mix tomatoes in blender until smooth. Add to pot along with soaked lentils and rice. Simmer soup for 10 minutes. Whisk flour together with 2 cups (500 ml) cold water, then pour through a strainer into the soup pot. Stir well and bring soup back to a boil, stirring until thickened.

Substitutions: Add some ground beef for a non-vegetarian version.

Ismaili Houssine, Chef
Sultan's Tent

Entrées

Green Curry Chicken

Serves: 2–3

1/2 cup	Coconut milk, canned	175 ml
	(reserve left over coconut milk for rice)	
1/2 cup	Water	175 ml
1 tbsp.	Green curry paste	15 ml
6 oz.	Boneless, skinless chicken breast, thinly sliced	175 g
6–8	Basil leaves, reserve 2 for garnish	6–8
1	Zucchini, sliced	1
1/2	Green pepper, sliced	1/2
1 tsp.	Salt (or to taste)	5 ml
1 tbsp.	Fish sauce	15 ml
	(if using fish sauce, omit the salt)	
1/2 tsp.	White sugar	2 ml

Garnish

2 tbsp.	Red pepper, chopped	30 ml
	or red chili, chopped for a hotter taste	
2 leaves	Chopped basil	2 leaves

Using a wok or a medium sauce pan, mix coconut milk and water with green curry paste. Add sliced chicken and basil and bring to a boil on medium heat. Boil for 2–3 minutes or until chicken slices are half cooked. Then add all vegetables and boil, stirring often for another 2–3 minutes. When chicken is cooked, add fish sauce or salt, and sugar. If the curry becomes too dry, add 1 more tbsp. (15 ml) coconut milk.

Serving suggestion: Serve at the table in a round serving bowl with garnish on top.

Substitutes: Shrimp or thinly sliced pork or beef are also suitable for this dish. Other vegetables may be used such as broccoli or Japanese eggplant. For root vegetables such as carrots, pre steam for 5 minutes. For a hotter dish, add a few slices of fresh chilies to the dish while cooking. If you can find Chaokoh coconut milk, it is highly recommended!

Coconut Rice

Serves: 2–3

1 cup	White long-grain rice	250 ml
	or Jasmine rice	
1 tsp.	Salt	5 ml
2 cups	Coconut milk, diluted with water	500 ml

If you have coconut milk left over from the Green Curry Chicken, dilute it with equal parts water and then make up the difference with water to reach 2 cups (500 ml). Mix all ingredients together and cook as you would normally cook rice.

Chef's Vanh, Sonthaya, Vida and Kalayarat
Thai-Sa-On

Alberta White Tail Venison and Ostrich Napoleon

Serves: 4

Layered with caramelized peach, wilted fresh greens and a toasted butter brioche, on peach and dried blueberry sauce and truffle scented celeriac purée.

Celeriac Purée

20 oz	Celeriac, raw	600 g
6 oz.	Butter	170 g
1 oz.	Pèrigord truffle	20 g

Celeriac is also called celery root. To cook, boil in salted water like potatoes until soft. Drain water and mix in a blender with the butter until smooth. Enhance flavour with fresh, diced French truffle. You can add truffle oil for more flavour.

White Tail Venison and Ostrich Napoleon

8 x 2 oz.	White tail venison, medallions cut from the striploin or leg (Denver Style)	8 x 55 g
4 x 2 oz.	Ostrich fan medallions	4 x 55 g
to taste	Fleur de sel	to taste
to taste	Fresh cracked white pepper	to taste

Sear medallions in a hot pan for 1–2 minutes on each side, rest in warm place 125°F (60°C) until serving time.

4 x 2 oz. portions	Brioche, sliced, seared **or** toasted, buttered	4 x 65 g portions

A Mixture of Fresh Greens

2 oz.	Basil, arugula, tatsoi, baby spinach and baby beet leaves	55 g

Peach Sauce

2	Fresh Okanagan Peaches, peeled and diced	2
2 tbsp.	Butter	30 ml
2 tbsp.	Dried blueberries from BC	30 ml
1/4 cup	Tawny Port, 10 years old	40 ml
1/2 cup	Venison jus	120 ml
2 tsp.	Butter, unsalted	10 ml

Caramelize the peaches in butter with dried blueberries. Flambé with Port wine. Simmer with venison jus for three minutes. Finish by adding 2 tsp. (10ml) of cold, unsalted butter. Stir and the sauce is ready.

Assembly of dish: Put two spoonfuls of celeriac purée onto each plate. Start to build the layers of the Napoleon beside the purée. The base of the Napoleon is a seared slice of buttered brioche. Then place one spoonful of the peach sauce on the baguette and a venison medallion on top. Then place the wilted greens on top. Slice the second venison diagonally into quarters and arranged nicely on the greens. The ostrich medallion is placed leaning against the Napoleon.

Serving suggestions: Serve your favourite vegetable and sautéed wild forest mushrooms. Recommended wines are Cru Burgundy, for example, Nuit St. George or Chambolle Mosign white.

Martin Heusser, Executive Chef
Owl's Nest

Pacific Halibut Steak
with Wildwood Amber Ale Sauce

Serves: 4

1	Onion	1
8	Black peppercorns	8
4 oz.	Butter	125 g
1/3 cup	Wildwood Amber beer	75 ml
1/4 cup	Cream	50 ml
1 tbsp.	Honey	15 ml
2 tbsp.	Soy sauce	30 ml
4 x 6 oz.	Halibut steaks	4 x 170 g
to taste	Salt and pepper	to taste

Sauté onions and peppercorns with half of the butter. Add the Wildwood Amber ale and reduce by 2/3. Add cream, honey and soy sauce. Reduce by 1/2 and whisk in the rest of the butter and strain.

Season halibut with salt and pepper; heat non-stick frying pan to medium-high heat. Cook halibut for about 3 minutes on each side.

Serving suggestions: Place halibut over a Warm Potato and Artichoke Salad (see facing page). Ladle Amber sauce around the halibut. For a wine suggestion, try Cline Zinfandel, California.

Josef Wiewer, Executive Chef
Wildwood

Warm Potato and Artichoke Salad

Serves: 4

20 oz.	Potatoes, small and cut in half	625 g
4	Fresh garlic cloves	4
2	Fresh sprigs of thyme	2
2	Bay leaves	2
2 cups	Olive oil	500 ml
1/2 tsp.	Salt	2 ml
1/4 tsp.	Black pepper	1 ml

Place all of the above ingredients in a small pot. Bring to a light boil, remove from heat. Cover with a lid and place pot in an oven at 350°F (180°C) for about 45 minutes or until potatoes are tender but still firm. (Potatoes can be made up to 3 days in advance and kept, tossed in the confit oil.)

12 oz.	Artichoke hearts cut into quarters	375 g
1 tbsp.	Capers	15 ml
1	Shallot, thinly sliced	1
4 tbsp.	Confit oil	60 ml
1 tbsp.	Rice wine vinegar	15 ml
to taste	Salt and pepper	to taste

To make salad, place potatoes in a bowl and mix with artichokes, capers, shallot, confit oil, rice wine vinegar, salt and pepper.

To serve: Warm on stovetop or in the oven to just over room temperature.

Josef Wiewer, Executive Chef
Wildwood

Chateaubriand for Two Baked in an "Igloo" of Coarse Sea Salt and Aromatic Herbs

Serves: 2

1 lb.	Naturally grown Galloway beef tenderloin (centre cut)	500 g
3 lbs.	Coarse sea salt	1.5 kg
1 tbsp.	Thyme, chopped	15 ml
1 tbsp.	Oregano, chopped	15 ml
1 tbsp.	Marjoram, chopped	15 ml
1 tbsp.	Rosemary, chopped	15 ml
1 tbsp.	Parsley, chopped	15 ml
1 tbsp.	Tarragon, chopped	15 ml
2	Vita egg whites	2
3/4 cup	Water	180 ml

Sear tenderloin over high heat on all sides. Blend all other ingredients into salt; adding water slowly so the salt can absorb the water and does not get too wet. There should not be any water at bottom of mixing bowl. In a frying pan, 8 inch in diametre (20 cm), make a thin bed of salt mix, place tenderloin on top and cover completely with the rest of salt. Cook at 400°F (200°C) for 22 minutes for medium rare. Take out of the oven and rest for 10–15 minutes before serving at table.

Crack the crust open at the table in front of your guest. Scrape off any salt crystals with back of a knife, before slicing the beef thinly on bias.

Serving suggestions: Serve beef at the table with two sauces, seasonal vegetables and your favourite potatoes. Sauce Béarnaise or Truffled Red Wine Jus are my recommended sauces to accompany the beef. Recommended wines are Argentinean Malbec or Amarone from Italy.

Martin Heusser, Executive Chef
Owl's Nest

Rosemary and Juniper Marinated Elk Steak
with a Wild Lingonberry Sauce

Serves: 4

4 x 6 oz.	Elk steak	4 x 170 g
1 tbsp.	Juniper berries, crushed	15 ml
1 tbsp.	Cracked black pepper	15 ml
4 tbsp.	Canola oil	60 ml
1 tsp.	Rosemary	5 ml
2 oz.	Red wine	50 ml
4 strips	Double smoked bacon	4 strips
3/4 cup	Wild lingonberries	175 ml
1 tbsp.	Honey	15 ml
4 oz.	Veal demi-glace	110 ml
1 tsp.	Madagascar green peppercorns	5 ml
1 tbsp.	Butter	15 ml
to taste	Salt and pepper	to taste

Marinate the elk steak with juniper berries, cracked black pepper and half of the rosemary with the oil for 24 hours. After marinating, wrap the elk with the slices of double smoked bacon. Heat the frying pan to medium–high heat; sear the steak quickly for approximately 3 minutes on each side (keep rare). Place elk on a warm plate, deglaze the pan with red wine and add the other ingredients except for butter. Reduce the sauce by half, whisk butter into the sauce being careful not to let the sauce boil.

Serving suggestion: Slice elk steak, arrange on the plate and drizzle with the sauce. An interesting wine accompaniment would be Freemark Abbey Cabernet Bosche, Napa Valley

Substitutions: Venison can be substituted for the elk. Wild lingonberries can be substituted with huckleberries (wild blueberries).

Josef Wiewer, Executive Chef
Wildwood

Grilled Alberta Buffalo Rib-Eye
with Mexican Potato Slaw, Fried Enchilada and Smoked Chipotle Chili Sauce

Serves: 4

4 x 10 oz.	Buffalo rib-eye	4 x 300 g

Chipotle Sauce

1 cup	Cranberry juice	250 ml
14 oz.	Small pears and juice, canned	400 ml
14 oz.	Apple juice	400 ml
1/2 cup	Apple cider vinegar	125 ml
4–6	Fresh thyme sprigs	4–6
2–3	Smoked chipotle peppers, canned, depending how spicy you like it	2–3
2 cups	Veal glaze	500 ml
2 cups	Chicken stock	500 ml

Bring all to a boil and simmer for 20 minutes. Remove thyme sprigs, and purée until smooth and then strain through sieve.

Potato Slaw and Dressing

1	Jicama*	1
1/2 cup	Carrot	125 ml
1/4 cup	Green zucchini	50 ml
1/4 cup	Red and yellow pepper	50 ml
1/4 cup	Extra virgin oil	50 ml
1	Lemon, zest and juice	1
1	Orange, zest and juice	1
1	Lime, zest and juice	1
1/2 tsp.	Red pepper flakes	2 ml
1/4 cup	Rice wine vinegar	50 ml
to taste	Salt and pepper	to taste

*Potato slaw, made with jicama, not potato, is a tradition in Mexico.

Julienne all the vegetables or use a mandeline. Mix remaining ingredients together and pour over julienned vegetables.

Enchilada Cheese Mix and Enchiladas

1/2 cup	Havarti cheese, grated	125 ml
1/2 cup	Smoked Gouda, grated	125 ml
1/2 cup	Asiago, grated	125 ml
1/4 cup	Green onion, chopped	50 ml
1 tbsp.	Black pepper	15 ml
to taste	Red chili flakes	to taste
4	Tortillas, 8 inch (20 cm)	4

Mix together the first 6 ingredients. For each flour tortilla, brush tortilla with olive oil, add 1/2 cup of cheese mix, roll tightly, and seal with a flour water mix.

Method

1. Prepare Chipotle Sauce
2. Make Potato Slaw and Enchiladas
3. Grill 4 buffalo rib-eye on BBQ. Cook until preferred temperature, season with salt and pepper, and let them sit for 5 minutes.
4. Heat Enchiladas on top of BBQ grill until the cheese melts.

Assembly of dish: Place sauce on bottom of plate, add slaw and grilled buffalo. Slice Enchiladas into three pieces and place on top of buffalo.

Substitutes: This recipe will also work well with beef or chicken.

Serving suggestions: Serve with 1999 St. Francis Cabernet from California.

Ken Canavan, Executive Chef
Cilantro

Sambuca Prawns

Serves: 1

1 tsp.	Butter	5 ml
2	Garlic cloves, minced	2
6	Large prawns	6
1 oz.	Sambuca	30 ml
1 cup	Cooked rice, plain or coconut	250 g
	Carrots cut into matchsticks	
	Fresh parsley	

Melt butter in frying pan, add garlic and caramelize. Add prawns and cook until prawns are pink. Add Sambuca and flambé.

Serving suggestions: Serve over warmed rice and garnish with carrots and fresh parsley. Be sure to pour all of the sauce over the rice — you'll love it!

Linda Crossley and Gerrit Visser, Chefs
Village Cantina

Cumin Roasted Spring Lamb
with Fresh Tomato and Cilantro Salsa

Serves: 4

4 x 7 oz.	Lamb racks **or** 20 oz. (600 g) boneless leg of lamb	4 x 200 g
2 tbsp.	Cumin, ground	30 ml
3 tsp.	Fennel seeds, ground	15 ml
3 tsp.	Coriander, ground	15 ml
4 cloves	Fresh garlic, chopped fine	4 cloves
2	Fresh orange zest, chopped fine	2
3 tsp.	Fresh rosemary, chopped fine	15 ml
to taste	Salt and black pepper	to taste

Clean lamb racks or roll leg to 2 inch (5 cm) diametre and tie. Combine all ingredients of lamb spices in a bowl. Season lamb with salt and black pepper. Crust lamb with spices. Roast lamb in 350°F (180°C) oven until internal temperature is 130°F (50–55°C). Test with a meat thermometer.

Fresh Tomato and Cilantro Salsa

3	Roma tomatoes, ripe and small cubed	3
2 tsp.	Cilantro, chopped coarse	10 ml
2 tsp.	Balsamic vinegar	10 ml
3 tsp.	Olive oil	15 ml

Sauté tomatoes in olive oil. Add cilantro. Toss with balsamic vinegar. Season with salt and black pepper.

Assembly of dish: Slice or carve lamb and serve with salsa.

Takashi Ito C.C.C., Executive Chef
The Fairmont Palliser

Crispy Cloved Spiced Squab and Foie Gras
with Balsamico, and Leek and Potato Cake

Serves: 4

2	Squab, large	2
	Canola oil for deep frying	
2	Leeks, whites only	2
7 tbsp.	Chicken stock	100 ml
4 x 1oz.	Sliced foie gras	4 x 30 g
2 tsp.	Aged Balsamico from Modena	10 ml
14 tbsp.	Reduced brown stock for sauce	200 ml

Remove the backbone and wings from the squab. Use bones to make brown stock. Steam breasts for 4 minutes. Cool at room temperature. Preheat hot oil to 375°F (190°C). Rub the squab in clove salt. Carefully add to the hot oil and fry for 2–3 minutes until rare and crispy. Remove and let rest. Season with clove salt.

Cut the leeks into rings and cook in the chicken stock. Drain and keep warm.

In a hot pan quickly sear foie gras for 20 seconds each side and keep warm.

Clove Salt

5	Whole cloves	5
1 tbsp.	Szechwan peppercorns	15 ml
5 tbsp.	Sea salt	75 ml

Toast all ingredients and grind.

Leek and Potato Cakes

1	Leek	1
1 tbsp.	Butter	15 ml
2	Yukon Gold potatoes	2

Dice the leek and sauté in butter until tender. Let cool. Cook the potatoes whole in salted water until half-done. Cool. Once the potatoes are cold, grate and place in a bowl. Mix in the leeks. Form the grated potatoes into cakes and chill until needed.

Brown your potato cakes in canola oil and roast in oven until golden and hot.

Assembly of dish: Place the hot and crispy potato cake in the centre of the plate. Spoon the leeks around potato cake. Drizzle the sauce (reduced brown stock) around leeks. Remove squab from the bone and place on top of potato cake. Place the foie gras on top of squab. Drizzle the balsamico on the squab and foie gras.

Substitutes: Quail can be used instead of squab — however the quails should be large or you must reduce the cooking time.

Michael Allemeier, Executive Chef
Teatro

Asian Cabbage Rolls

Yields: 30–40 rolls

2	Cabbage, large heads	2

Filling

8 cups	Rice, freshly cooked	2 litres
2 cups	Fresh cilantro, chopped	500 ml
2 cups	Green onion, sliced	500 ml
1 tsp. each	Garlic, shallots and fresh ginger	5 ml each
1 cup	Red pepper, diced	250 ml
2 cups	Black beans, cooked	500 ml
1/8 tsp. each	Salt and pepper	0.5 ml each
1/2 cup	Mushrooms, slivered	125 ml
2 tbsp.	Lime juice	30 ml

Topping

8	Tomatoes, medium, diced	8
1/8 cup	Sesame seeds	30 ml
1/4 cup	Pickled ginger, chopped	50 ml
2 cups	Soy sauce	500 ml
1 1/2 cups	Red wine vinegar	375 ml
1/4 cup	Sesame oil	50 ml

Assembling the rolls: Blanch the two large heads of cabbage until leaves start to separate from the head. Remove the leaves and place in ice water as they are done. When all the leaves are done, remove the thickest part of the backbone of the leaf at the bottom, leaving the rest to help roll. Once you have cut the backbone out put a spoonful of filling in the middle. Pull the bottom over the filling and pull each side in and roll tightly. Put the rolls in an ovenproof dish placing the rolls very tightly together. Put the topping on and cover with foil and bake for 20–30 min.

Serving suggestion: Add some ground meat.

Michelle Ducie, Associate Chef
Pickled Parrot

Wild Mushroom Ravioli

Serves: 6 as a main course, 15 as an appetizer

2 cups	Mushrooms (a mix of your favourites), chopped	500 ml
1 tsp. each	Garlic and shallots, minced	5 ml each
1 tbsp.	Rosemary, chopped	15 ml
1 tsp.	Balsamic vinegar	5 ml
1/4 tsp.	Salt and pepper	1 ml
1/4 cup	Gorgonzola cheese	50 ml
2	Eggs	2
	Olive oil	
1 package	Small wonton wrappers	1 package

Sauté mushrooms with garlic and shallots in olive oil. Add rosemary, vinegar, salt and pepper. Remove from heat and slowly incorporate the cheese. When the mixture is cooled, add one egg — this will help bind the mixture. Use the second egg to create an egg wash by mixing in equal parts of water. (This is used to seal the wraps.) Place 1 tsp. (5 ml) of filling in the centre of one wonton wrap, egg wash the edges and place another wrapper on top and press edges together. Boil a pot of water (as you would for pasta). Slowly drop ravioli in the boiling water. They will start to float and become slightly transparent, remove and drizzle olive oil on top of ravioli.

Serving suggestion: Garnish with some freshly grated cheese.

Michelle Ducie, Associate Chef
Pickled Parrot

Elk Steaks
with Green Peppercorn Sauce

Serves: 4

4 x 6 oz.	Steaks from leg or loin	4 x 170 g
2 tbsp.	Olive oil	30 ml
1 tbsp.	Butter	15 ml
to taste	Salt and pepper	to taste
	Flour	

Heat oil and butter in a heavy bottomed frying pan over medium–high heat. Season steaks with salt and pepper, dip into flour and shake off excess. Fry to your liking. Remove meat, set aside on a plate to catch the juices and keep warm.

Green Peppercorn Sauce

1	Shallot, finely chopped	1
2 tsp.	Green peppercorns	10 ml
2 tbsp.	Dry white wine	30 ml
1 cup	Whipping cream	250 ml
1 tsp.	Dijon mustard	5 ml
to taste	Salt	to taste

Discard frying oil, leaving 1 tbsp. (15 ml). Sauté shallot and green peppercorns briefly. Pour wine into the pan, boil down liquid to 1/4 and stir in cream and mustard. Reduce again until sauce becomes slightly thick. Add meat juices to the sauce. Adjust seasoning with salt if necessary.

Serving suggestion: Arrange steaks on warmed plates and pour sauce over. Serve with green vegetables and homemade French fries.

Substitute: Buffalo, beef (do not flour), pork chops and all the deer family.

Klaus Wöckinger, Chef/Owner
Big Rock Grill

Fiery Dragon Noodle Stir-Fry

Serves: 2–3

1/4 cup	Chicken breast, thinly sliced	50 g
1 tsp.	Ginger, freshly grated	5 ml
1	Garlic clove, crushed	1
1	Medium red pepper, cut into thin strips	1
1	Medium green pepper, cut into thin strips	1
1	Medium onion, cut into thin strips	1
1 lb.	Shanghai noodles, cooked (found in refrigerated section of grocery store)	450 g
3 tbsp.	Soy sauce	45 ml
1 tbsp.	Oyster sauce	15 ml
2 tbsp.	Chili garlic sauce	30 ml
1 1/2 tbsp.	Sugar	25 ml
2 tbsp.	Canola oil	30 ml

Heat oil in a wok, add ginger, garlic and chicken and stir-fry for 1 minute. Add peppers, onion and noodles and stir-fry for 30 seconds. Add remaining ingredients and continue cooking for 1 more minute stirring constantly. Transfer to serving bowls and eat with chopsticks.

Gary Hennessey, Chef
Open Sesame

Fish Tagine
(Fish Stew)

Serves: 4

1	Red pepper, julienned	1
1	Green pepper, julienned	1
2	Carrots, julienned	2
4	Potato quarters, partially cooked	4
1–1 1/2 cups	Fresh or canned tomatoes, diced	250–375 ml
4	Green or black olives	4
1	Preserved lemon (see below)	1
2 tbsp.	Pure extra virgin olive oil	30 ml
2–3 tbsp.	Water	30–45 ml
	Fillets of sole, tiger prawns or substitutes	
1/4 tsp.	Cumin	1 ml
1/4 tsp.	Paprika	1 ml
pinch each	Salt and cayenne pepper	pinch each
1–3	Garlic cloves, crushed	1–3
to taste	Cilantro or parsley	to taste
	Fresh lemon juice	
	Fresh bread	

In a saucepan or frying pan (also suitable for the oven), sauté peppers, carrots and potatoes with tomatoes, olives and preserved lemon with water and olive oil for five minutes. Add desired fish and simmer for five additional minutes.

Add spices and garlic, sprinkle cilantro or parsley on top and simmer in oven at medium heat for 10–15 minutes. Squeeze fresh lemon juice on top and serve with fresh bread.

Moroccan Preserved Lemon

Cut a lemon almost in half and then almost in quarters. Place in a small bowl with water to cover and add 1 tsp. (5 ml) of salt. Cover and keep in refrigerator for at least one week. Cut in wedges and add to sauce for a distinctive soft Moroccan lemon flavour.

Ismaili Houssine, Chef
Sultan's Tent

Hare Tagine
(Rabbit Stew)

Serves: 3–4

| 1 | Rabbit, de-boned and cut into small pieces | 1 |

Marinade

4	Garlic cloves, minced	4
1 tbsp.	Cilantro, finely chopped	15 ml
1/2 tsp.	Ginger, ground	2 ml
1/4 tsp.	Salt	1 ml
1/4 tsp.	Black pepper	1 ml
1/4 tsp.	Paprika	1 ml
4 tbsp.	Extra virgin olive oil	60 ml

Coat rabbit with marinade, cover and cool in refrigerator for half an hour.

Sauce

4 tbsp.	Olive oil	60 ml
1	Yellow or red onion, finely chopped	1
1–2	Fresh tomatoes, finely chopped	1–2
1–2	Preserved lemon wedges (see previous page) **or** 4–5 olives any kind, if preferred	1–2
1 cup	Water	250 ml
	Julienned strips of vegetables like carrots, zucchini, peppers are optional	

Sauté marinated rabbit with oil and onion for 15 minutes on top of stove. Add tomatoes, vegetables of your choice and lemon wedges and simmer in 375–400°F (200°C) oven for 15–20 minutes.

Serving suggestion: Serve and eat Moroccan style by tearing pieces of bread and dipping up the meat and sauce with fingers.

Ismaili Houssine, Chef
Sultan's Tent

Harvest Beef Stew
with Black Amber Ale

Serves: 4

1 1/2 lbs.	Boneless stewing beef, cubed	700 g
4 tbsp.	Canola oil	60 ml
to taste	Salt and pepper	to taste
1	Large onion, finely chopped	1
2	Garlic cloves, finely chopped	2
4 tbsp.	Flour	60 ml
1 bottle	Black Amber Ale	1 bottle
2	Bay leaves	2
1 tsp.	Thyme	5 ml
1 tsp.	Oregano	5 ml
2 tsp.	Worcestershire sauce	10 ml
1 1/2 cups	Beef bouillon	375 ml
3	Medium carrots, cubed	3
1/2	Turnip, cubed	1/2
1/2	Small white cabbage, large dice	1/2
4	Small potatoes, peeled and cubed	4

In a large saucepan heat oil over medium high heat. Season beef with salt and pepper, and brown. Remove meat and sauté onion and garlic until soft, add flour and stir for 1 minute. Slowly pour in the beer. Return meat, add seasoning and simmer for 1 hour 15 minutes, adding beef bouillon as needed. Stir in vegetables and cook for an additional 30 minutes. Adjust seasoning and serve with a fresh baguette.

Klaus Wöckinger, Chef/Owner
Big Rock Grill

Northern Pike Baked in Tinfoil
with Meadow Herbs

Serves: 4

2 1/2 lbs.	Pike	1.2 kg
to taste	Salt and pepper	to taste
1	Lemon	1
2 cups	Cabbage, shredded (white Savoy or Chinese)	500 ml
1	Celery stalk, large and sliced	1
1	Carrot, medium shredded	1
1/2	Onion, small sliced	1/2
1/2 cup	Meadow herbs (young dandelion leaves, watercress, wild garlic, sorrel, etc.) **or** coarsely chopped parsley, scallions, chives and leeks	125 ml
4 tbsp.	Light beer or wine	60 ml
4 tbsp.	Butter	60 ml
2 tbsp.	Olive oil	30 ml

Scrub fish thoroughly on the outside. Remove all fins and gills. Clean under running water and dry with a paper towel. Preheat oven to 400°F (200°C). Coat heavy duty tinfoil with 1 tbsp. (15ml) butter and place on a baking sheet. Season fish inside and out with salt and pepper. Place fish onto foil, sprinkle with juice of 1/2 lemon. Combine all vegetables and herbs. Place some mixture into cavity and arrange remainder on top of fish. Squeeze other half of lemon juice over top. Add beer or wine, butter and oil. Seal foil securely so no steam can escape. Place into oven for about 30 minutes.

Serving suggestions: Remove meat from fish, using soup spoon starting along the backside of fish. Arrange on warm plates and serve with parsley potatoes.

Substitute: Pickerel, perch or salmon

Klaus Wöckinger, Chef/Owner
Dante's

Pan Fried Salmon
with Potato Pecan Pancakes, Shittake Mushrooms and Tomato Ginger Salsa

Serves: 3

3 oz.	Salmon, boneless portions 3 each	90 g
to taste	Salt and pepper	to taste

Sprinkle with salt and pepper and pan fry to medium rare.

Potato Pecan Pancakes

1 lb.	Yukon Gold potatoes, baked and grated	450 g
3	Eggs	3
3	Egg whites	3
3 tbsp.	Corn starch	45 ml
1 cup	Pecans, chopped	250 ml
to taste	Salt and pepper	to taste
	Clarified butter, for frying	

Mix ingredients together and let rest for 1 hour.

Pan fry on a hot skillet with clarified butter until edges turn lightly golden brown.

Shittake Mushrooms

Shitake mushrooms, sliced
Olive oil
Butter
Salt and pepper

Use the best, not too big or too small — just right. Sauté the mushrooms in equal amounts of olive oil and butter. Season lightly with salt and pepper to taste.

Tomato Ginger Salsa

6	Medium tomatoes, 1/4 inch (5 mm) dice	6
1	Small red onion, 1/4 inch (5 mm) dice	1
1/4 cup	Ginger, fine dice	50 ml
1/2 oz.	Rice vinegar	15 ml
1 oz.	Virgin olive oil	25 ml
1 tsp.	Garlic, fine dice	5 ml
1 tsp.	Parsley, chopped	5 ml
to taste	Salt and pepper	to taste

Combine above ingredients and mix thoroughly.

Assembly of dish: Rest salmon on top of potato pecan pancake and spoon salsa over both. Place mushrooms around the outside of salmon to form a ring.

Lance Irvine, Sous-Chef
Smuggler's Inn

Paella Valencia

Serves: 4

1	Chicken	1
1/4 cup	Olive oil	50 ml
8 oz.	Bacon, diced	250 g
1/2 lb.	Tomatoes, peeled and chopped	250 g
1	Garlic petal	1
6–8 oz.	Green beans or peas, cooked	170–225 g
1	Artichoke (optional)	1
2 tsp.	Pimento	10 ml
1 1/2 cups	Rice, uncooked	375 ml
1 pint	Water	500 ml
pinch	Saffron	pinch
6 oz.	Eel, uncooked	170 g
12	Snails, canned jumbo	12
6 oz.	Crawfish	170 g
to taste	Salt	to taste

Cube chicken and salt lightly. In large frying pan heat oil and fry chicken with bacon for 5 minutes. Add the tomatoes, garlic, green beans or peas, artichokes, pimento and rice. Mix gently for 5 minutes, then add water. When all is boiling, add a little saffron, eel, snails and salt. When rice is half cooked add crawfish and finish cooking slowly in oven at 275°F (140°C).

Jake Kirchner, Executive Chef
Carver's Steakhouse, Sheraton

Pan Seared Halibut
with White Wine Crispy Caper Butter

Serves: 1

6 oz.	Filet of halibut, each	170 g
2 tbsp.	Vegetable oil	30 ml
4 oz.	Potato disks	120 g
5	Asparagus stems	5
to taste	Coarse salt and white pepper	to taste
1 oz.	White Wine Crispy Caper butter	30 ml
pinch	Chili flakes, ground	pinch

Heat 1 tbsp. (15 ml) of vegetable oil in Teflon-coated pan until hot. Sauté halibut on both sides until lightly browned around edges. Season with coarse salt and white pepper and place in preheated 375°F (190°C) oven for 8 minutes. In a roasting pan, heat potato disks and asparagus with 1 tbsp. (15 ml) vegetable oil and salt and pepper. When tender, stack the potato disks in the centre of a dinner plate and lay asparagus on disks in a criss-cross fashion. Place halibut on top and drizzle with caper butter. Sprinkle with ground chili flakes to taste.

White Wine Crispy Caper Butter

1 tsp.	Capers, chopped	5 ml
2 tbsp.	Butter	30 ml
1 tbsp.	White wine	15 ml
to taste	Salt and pepper	to taste

Stir-fry capers in butter and season to taste. Add white wine and reduce by half.

Serving suggestion: Garnish with a lemon wedge and cilantro sprig.

Steve Little, Executive Chef
4th Street Rose

Pulled Duck Confit on Taber Corn-Thyme Griddle Cakes

Serves: 8

Duck Confit

3	Duck, fresh with legs attached	3
to taste	Kosher salt and cracked black pepper	to taste
4	Fresh thyme, sprigs	4
1	Bay leaf	1
4 cups	Rendered duck fat	1 litre

Liberally rub the duck with salt and pepper and let sit for 1 day in the refrigerator.

Sear the duck, fat side down in a hot skillet to caramelize the skin, draining off and saving the fat. Place the duck in a shallow pot and add the duck fat and remnants of the searing. Add the thyme and bay leaf, melt the fat over a medium heat and bring to a simmer. Cover and place in a 325°F (150°C) oven for 2–3 hours. Take out and allow to cool.

With your hands, pull off the outer layer of skin and pull the meat off the bone and lightly shred it into strips. Strain the warm duck fat through a fine sieve or coffee filter to take out any particles from the confit. To reserve the meat for another day, place it back into the strained duck fat, making sure it is fully submersed and keep in the refrigerator for up to 1 month.

Cranberry-Balsamic and Molasses Syrup

2 cups	Balsamic vinegar, good quality	500 ml
3 tbsp.	Molasses	45 ml
1/4 cup	Cranberries, frozen	50 ml
1 sprig	Fresh rosemary	1 sprig

Place all ingredients into a small, non-reactive saucepan and reduce by 2/3 or until it turns into a syrup consistency. Strain and keep at room temperature.

Taber Corn-Thyme Griddle Cakes

1 1/2 cups	Corn kernels, preferably fresh	375 ml
1/3 cup	Cornmeal	75 ml
1/2 tsp.	Kosher salt	2 ml
1/3 cup	All-purpose flour	75 ml
1/2 tsp.	Baking powder	2 ml
1/8 tsp.	White pepper	1 ml
2	Egg yolks, large	2
2/3 cup	Heavy cream	150 ml
2 tbsp.	Unsalted butter, melted	30 ml
2 tbsp.	Fresh thyme, chopped	30 ml
	Thyme sprigs for garnish	
	Vegetable oil for frying	

Cook the corn kernels in a pot of boiling water until tender, about 2 minutes. Drain. In bowl, combine the cornmeal, salt, flour, baking powder, pepper and mix. In another bowl, whisk together the egg yolks and cream. Pour in dry ingredients and mix until smooth.

Add the butter, blanched corn and thyme and let sit for 30 minutes. Heat a non-stick skillet or griddle to medium heat with 1 tsp. (5 ml) of oil to lightly coat pan and drop 1 heaping teaspoon of the batter at a time onto the surface. Press down with the spoon to form circular disks. Flip the cakes after about 1 minute or when the edges start to brown. When golden brown on both sides, remove the cakes and place them on paper towel to drain off excess grease. Keep warm in a 150°F (65°C) oven until you are ready to assemble the appetizers.

Assembly of dish: Lay out the corn cakes on a plate or platter. Warm the confit slightly in a sauté pan or in the oven. Mound about 1 1/2 tablespoons (20 ml) of the confit in the centre of each cake. Drizzle a touch of the cranberry-balsamic and molasses syrup over the confit. Garnish each cake with a small sprig of thyme and a sundried cranberry. Serve and enjoy!

Chris Grafton, Chef
The Ranche Restaurant

Russian River Grilled Chicken

Serves: 6

6 x 6 oz.	Chicken breasts	6 x 170 g

Grill stuffed chicken breasts skin side down for approx. 2 minutes. Flip and grill for another 2 minutes.

Spread red pepper tapanade over the skin side and bake in preheated oven at 375°F (190°C) for final cooking, approximately 12 minutes.

Stuffing Mix

2 oz.	Goat cheese	55 g
1/2 lb.	Shallots, roasted	225 g
4 oz.	Garlic, roasted	115 g
4 oz.	Fresh basil	115 g

Coarsely chop and mix together (do not purée) and stuff chicken breasts.

Tapanade

2	Red peppers	2
to taste	Salt and pepper	to taste

Purée and spoon over chicken breasts.

Assembly of dish: Place demi-glace on a dinner plate, covering the entire inside to the rim. Place 3 oz. (85 g) of field greens in the centre of the plate. Place potato rösti directly on top of the greens (this is to protect the rösti from touching the demi-glace and becoming soggy). Cut the chicken breast in half and shingle onto one side of the rösti.

Alternative for demi-glace: Serve your own homemade gravy.

Potato Rösti

Serves: 6

4 lbs.	Yukon gold potatoes, cut into frites	2 kg
2 lbs.	Sweet potatoes, cut into frites	1 kg
4 oz.	Fresh chiffonade of basil	120 ml
4 oz.	Goat cheese	120 ml
4 oz.	Cream cheese	120 ml
2 oz.	Sour cream	60 ml
2 oz.	Garlic purée	60 ml
2 tbsp.	Salt	30 ml
2 tbsp.	Pepper	30 ml
	Vegetable oil for frying	

Mix all ingredients well. Heat a small Teflon-coated frying pan with 2 tbsp. (30 ml) vegetable oil. Add 4 oz. (120 ml) of rösti mix and form into rounds. Sauté until brown on both sides. Edges should be crispy. Lay out on a parchment lined sheet pan to drain and serve immediately.

Steve Little, Executive Chef
4th Street Rose

Rainbow Trout
with White Wine Butter Sauce

Serves: 4

4 x 10 oz.	Trout	4 x 300 g
to taste	Salt and pepper	to taste
3 tbsp.	Butter	45 ml

Preheat oven to 375°F (190°C). Clean fish under running water, dry with paper towel. Season inside and out with salt and pepper. Melt butter in a frying or roasting pan and bake fish for about 15 minutes

White Wine Butter Sauce

1/2 cup	White wine	125 ml
4 tbsp.	Butter, cold	60 ml
	Flour to coat butter	
2 tbsp.	Capers	30 ml
1	Small tomato, diced	1
1	Small lemon, peeled and diced	1
1 tbsp.	Parsley, chopped	15 ml

Place a medium-sized sauce pan over high heat. Add white wine and bring to a boil. Reduce to half the volume. Lightly coat cold butter pieces with flour and stir into boiling wine using a wire whisk. Add all other ingredients. Bring back to a boil and serve.

Serving Suggestion: Arrange fish on warm plate, spoon sauce on top and sprinkle with parsley. Serve with potatoes or rice and salad.

Substitute: Most types of fish or fillets of fish.

Klaus Wöckinger, Chef/Owner
Dante's

Sesame Crusted Salmon
with Ginger Miso Beurre Blanc

Serves: 8

Salmon

8 x 6 oz.	Salmon fillets	8 x 170 g
2 tbsp.	Hoisin sauce	30 ml
1/4 cup	Sesame seeds, toasted	60 ml
1/4 cup	Olive oil	60 ml

Heat pan over medium–high heat with half of the olive oil. Season salmon with salt and pepper. Brown each salmon piece, skin side up, for 30 seconds. Remove and place seared side up on a baking sheet, lined with parchment paper. Once all salmon has been seared, lightly coat with Hoisin sauce. Sprinkle with the toasted sesame seeds and bake in oven at 350°F (180°C) for approximately 7 minutes. Remove and let stand 2 minutes before serving.

Ginger Miso Beurre Blanc

2 tbsp.	White wine vinegar	25 ml
1 tsp.	White wine	5 ml
2 tsp.	Shallots, minced	10 ml
1 tsp.	Miso paste	5 ml
2 tsp.	Ginger, minced	10 ml
8 oz.	Butter, chilled and cut into pieces	250 g

Combine the vinegar, white wine, shallots, miso and ginger in small saucepan. Reduce until almost dry (au sec). Over low heat, whisk in butter, a few pieces at a time. Once all butter has been incorporated, remove sauce from heat. Strain through a fine chinois (sieve).

to taste	Lemon juice	to taste
1 tsp.	Salt	5 ml
1/2 tsp.	White pepper	2 ml

Whisk a few drops of lemon juice in at a time. Add salt and pepper and adjust to taste. Serve at once with salmon.

C.R. (Bob) Matthews, Executive Chef
La Chaumière Restaurant

Venison and Four Cheese Strudel

Serves: 8

Strudel

1 tbsp.	Olive oil to sauté mushrooms	15 ml
4/5 cup	Sliced mushrooms	200 g
3 cups	Root vegetables, julienned and sautéed	750 ml
14 oz.	Venison pastrami, sliced	400 g
9 oz.	Assorted cheeses (Port Salut, Stilton, Brie, Cambozola, etc.)	250 g
2 cups	Mizuna greens or spinach, sautéed	500 g
2 oz.	Fresh basil	50 g
2 oz.	Fresh thyme	50 g
2 oz.	Fresh parsley	50 g
3	Garlic cloves, chopped	3
2	Large shallots, chopped	2
to taste	Salt and black pepper	to taste
	Butter, melted for brushing	
1 pack	Phyllo pastry	1 pack

Sauté mushrooms in olive oil until slightly browned. Add vegetables and season, take off heat and allow to drain thoroughly. In a large bowl combine the cool, drained mushroom mixture. Add the venison pastrami, cheese, mizuna and all the flavourings. Season well and place in refrigerator to keep cool until ready to roll strudel.

Place one sheet of phyllo lengthways on table and brush lightly with melted butter. Fold sheet in half creating a square, place 1/8 of filling on the bottom. Take the bottom of the sheet and fold it over the filling. Gently pull back on the roll to tighten it. Roll once more then fold ends into the centre, creating the strudel. Repeat until all filling is used up. Finish rolling, brush with melted butter and keep covered in refrigerator until ready to bake at 350°F (180°C) for 15–20 minutes or until golden brown.

Apple Compote

1 tbsp.	Olive oil	15 ml
3	Large Granny Smith apples	3
6	Oranges, juiced	6
to taste	Salt and black pepper	to taste
to taste	Cilantro, fresh, chopped	to taste

Peel and core apples. Cut into large dice. In a large pan on high heat, add apples with olive oil. Allow apples to caramelize to a deep brown. Add orange juice and allow to reduce to almost dry. Purée and season with salt, pepper and cilantro.

Substitutes: Instead of venison pastrami use ham or other cold cuts.

C.R. (Bob) Matthews, Executive Chef
La Chaumière Restaurant

Venison Skewer

Serves: 4

21 oz.	Tender meat from leg or loin	600 g
1 tbsp.	Olive oil	15 ml
1	Green bell pepper	1
1/2	Onion	1/2
3	Bacon slices	3
12	Mushrooms	12
4 tbsp.	Olive or peanut oil	60 ml
to taste	Salt and pepper	to taste

Cut meat, green pepper, onion and bacon into bite-sized pieces. Heat oil in a frying pan over medium heat. Sauté green pepper, onion and bacon until they are soft, remove and set aside.

To place on skewers, start with meat, then one piece of each: bacon, onion, green pepper and mushroom. Start over again until all meat is used. (Remember to start and finish the skewer with meat; otherwise, pieces will fall off during cooking.)

Heat oil in a large frying pan over high heat. Season skewers and fry to your liking, or brush with oil and place them on a very hot grill.

Serving suggestions: Serve with curried rice (see facing page) spooned onto the middle of warmed plates. Strip off skewer with a fork onto rice. A mixed salad will complement this dish.

Substitute: Different types of meat such as beef, liver and chicken can be mixed, as long as they are tender.

Klaus Wöckinger, Chef/Owner
Big Rock Grill

ATHICH

Curried Rice
with Pineapple

Serves: 4–6

2 tbsp.	Onion, chopped	30 ml
2 tbsp.	Butter	30 ml
1 cup	Long grain rice	250 ml
2 tsp.	Curry powder	10 ml
2 cups	Water	500 ml
2 tsp.	Salt	10 ml
4	Pineapple rings, fresh or canned	4

In a saucepan, sauté onion with butter over medium heat. When onion is soft but not brown, add rice and curry; sauté for 1 minute. Increase heat, add water and salt and bring to a boil. Cover and turn heat down to low. Simmer for 25 minutes, stirring the rice once towards the end of the cooking time. Cut pineapple rings into small pieces and mix into rice.

Klaus Wöckinger, Chef/Owner
Big Rock Grill

Steak au Poivre

Veal Stock

Yields: 8 cups (2 litres)

10 lbs.	Marrow veal bones, oven roasted	4.5 kg
	Onion	
	Carrots	
	Leeks	
	Celery	
	Bouquet garni	
10 qts.	Cold water	10 litres

Roast marrowbones in oven at 450°F (230°C) for 2 1/2 hours, adding onion and carrots towards the end of the cooking time. Degrease and deglaze the pan. Add remaining vegetables, bouquet garni, cold water and simmer for about 5 hours. Strain and reduce to 1/4. Degrease once more and reserve.

Steak

Serves: 1

8 oz.	Striploin steak (Galloway by choice)	225 g
1 tbsp.	Oil for frying	15 ml
to taste	Black pepper, coarsely ground	to taste
1 oz.	Cognac	30 g
3 oz.	Cream (35%)	85 g
2 soup sp.	Veal stock	150 ml
to taste	Salt	to taste

Season steak with pepper and sear both sides to your liking. Discard the oil and flambé with cognac. Put the meat aside. Add cream with veal stock and reduce by about 1/2. Season with salt and pepper to taste. When sauce has thickened enough, return the strip loin to pan and finish cooking to your liking.

Serving suggestion: Serve with french fries

Patrice Durandeau, Owner and Dan McKinley, Chef
Fleur de Sel

Smuggler's Chicken Kiev

Serves: 4

4 x 6 oz.	Large chicken breasts halved, deboned and skinless	4 x 170 g
1/2 tsp.	Seasoning salt	2 ml
to taste	Fresh cracked pepper	to taste
4 tbsp.	Butter, soft	60 ml
1 cup	Long grain rice, cooked	250 ml
1	Garlic clove, minced	1
4 sprigs	Parsley, chopped	4 sprigs
8 stems	Chives, chopped	8 stems

On sanitized cutting board lay chicken breasts down (skin side down), season with seasoning salt and a little fresh cracked pepper and refrigerate. Combine remaining ingredients, divide into four and roll into cylinders. Place each filling cylinder onto a chicken breast, roll up firmly and freeze for four hours.

Breading

2 oz.	Milk	55 g
1	Egg	1
1/2 tsp.	Seasoning salt	2 ml
3 tbsp.	Flour	45 ml
1 1/4 cup	Bread crumbs	550 ml
1/4 cup	Canola oil,	50 ml

Combine milk, egg and salt and beat well. Set breading station — flour first, egg wash second and bread crumbs third. Roll partially frozen chicken breasts in flour, dip into egg wash, then roll into bread crumbs. Be sure to press firmly. Repeat for a thicker coating.

Heat skillet on medium heat with 1/4 cup (50 ml) canola oil. Gently fry each breast rolling carefully with tongs. Once lightly browned, transfer to baking dish and bake in a preheated 350°F (180°C) oven for 18–20 minutes. Serve at once with fresh lemon, boiled potatoes and green vegetables. Enjoy!

David Clearwater, Chef
Smuggler's Inn

Diner Meat Loaf

Serves: 6–8

1 cup	Carrot, roasted and diced	250 ml
1 cup	Parsnips, roasted and diced	250 ml
to taste	Olive oil, salt and pepper	to taste
32 oz.	Veal, ground	1 kg
32 oz.	Beef, ground	1 kg
3	Eggs	3
1/2 cup	Green onions, diced	125 ml
1 tsp.	Ground cumin	5 ml
1 tsp.	Coriander	5 ml
1 tsp.	Mustard powder	5 ml
2 tsp.	Worcestershire sauce	10 ml
1 tsp.	Hot sauce	5 ml
3 tsp.	Salt	15 ml
3 tsp.	Green pepper corns, ground	15 ml
2 tsp.	Fresh garlic, chopped	10 ml

To roast vegetables dice carrots and parsnips, toss with olive oil, salt and pepper. Place on sheet pan and roast at 350°F (180°C) oven until tender or approximately 30 minutes.

Mix all ingredients together well and place in two loaf pans, 5 x 8 inches (12 x 20 cm) and bake at 450°F (230°C) until internal temperature is 140°F (60°C). Let cool in the pans.

Serving suggestions: Cut the meat loaf into thick slices and serve with mashed potatoes. Smother everything with beef gravy and serve with grilled or roasted tomatoes on the side.

Dwayne Ennest, Chef
Diner Deluxe

Desserts & Special Drinks

Mousse au Chocolate et Whiskey

Serves: 12

8 oz.	Dark semi-sweet Callebaut chocolate	225 g
8 oz.	Milk Callebaut chocolate	225 g
2 oz.	Salted butter	50 g
2 cups	Cream (35%)	500 ml
6	Eggs, separated	6
pinch	Salt	pinch
2 oz.	Granulated sugar	50 g
2 oz.	Jack Daniels whiskey	50 ml

Chill 12 dessert glass bowls or large crystal bowl in the refrigerator. Melt both chocolates and the butter in a double boiler. Whisk cream and egg whites (including a pinch of salt) separately until peaks form. Beat the egg yolks with the sugar until white "ribbon stage."

Pour the melted chocolate in a separate container, add the whiskey, then fold in the beaten egg yolks followed by half of the whipped cream, half of the egg whites and repeat again with the rest of whipped cream and egg whites and pour mixture into chilled glasses.

Note: It tastes even better the next day. So if possible, prepare a day ahead.

Patrice Durandeau, Owner and Dan McKinley, Chef
Fleur de Sel

Tapioca Pudding and Honeydew Melon

Serves: 4

1/2 cup	Seed tapioca	125 ml
14 oz.	Coconut milk, canned	400 ml
1 cup	White sugar	250 ml
1 cup	Fresh honeydew melon, cubed	250 ml

Soak tapioca in cold water for 4 hours. Use enough water to cover tapioca sufficiently; about 1 cup (250 ml). Heat coconut milk in small pot on medium heat until boiling. Add sugar. Rinse tapioca and pour into coconut milk; continue to cook and stir for about 5-10 minutes. When tapioca is cooked, it will turn transparent. If the mixture becomes too thick while cooking, dilute with a bit of cold water. Cool the mixture in the fridge and serve with fresh fruit. If you want to serve the pudding thinner, stir in some extra 2% milk.

Serving suggestion: Serve in individual bowls.

Substitutions: You can substitute mango, strawberry, or banana for the melon.

Bingo Chung, Helen Chung, Executive Chefs
The King and I

Maple Poached Pear Strudel

Serves: 4

Poached Pears

2–3	Pears, peeled and cored	2–3
2 cups	Water	500 ml
1/4 cup	Maple syrup	50 ml
1/4 cup	Brown sugar	50 ml
1	Cinnamon stick or pinch of ground cinnamon	1

Slice each pear in half, then each half into approximately eight pieces. Bring water, maple syrup, sugar and cinnamon to a simmer in a medium-sized saucepan. Add pears and poach until tender. They are nice when a bit crispy; however it is up to you.

Caramel Sauce

1 cup	Granulated sugar	250 ml
1/4 cup	Water	50 ml
1 tbsp.	Lemon juice	15 ml
4 tbsp.	Butter	60 ml
3 cups	Whipping cream	750 ml

Heat sugar, water and lemon juice over medium heat, stirring to dissolve the sugar. Once the sugar is dissolved, clean the sides of the pot with a pastry brush dipped in water. Turn heat to high, without stirring. Allow the sugar to turn a caramel colour. Once you have reached this stage, stir in the butter one tablespoon at a time until it is completely blended. After all the butter is incorporated, add the cream slowly while continuing to stir. Be careful, the cream will make the mixture bubble and steam profusely. Once all the cream has been added, let the sauce simmer over low heat for approximately 5 minutes without boiling. Allow the sauce to cool.

Strudel Assembly

Pre-heat oven to 350°F (180°C)

4 sheets	Phyllo pastry	4 sheets
	Melted butter	
	Poached pears	
	Caramel sauce	
	Sun-dried cranberries or raisins	

Cut the phyllo in half, forming eight pieces. Brush each piece with the melted butter. Place 4–6 pieces of pear on the bottom of each piece. Sprinkle with cranberries. Drizzle about 2 tsp. (10 ml) of sauce over each. Fold in the sides of the phyllo and butter again. Starting from the bottom roll the pears in the phyllo. Bake in a 350°F (180°C) oven for 8–12 minutes, or until golden brown.

Serving suggestion: Serve warm with ice cream and the remaining sauce.

Tanya Heck, Pastry Chef
Wildwood

Dutch Apple Pie

Serves: 6

Single pastry, 11 inches (28 cm)

Apple Filling

8 cups	Golden Delicious or Granny Smith apples	2 litres
2 cups	Sour cream	500 ml
1 cup	Sugar	250 ml
1/2 cup	Flour	125 ml
2	Eggs	2
1 tsp.	Pure vanilla extract	5 ml

Brown Sugar Topping

1/2 cup	Brown sugar	125 ml
1/4 cup	Walnuts, chopped	50 ml
1/4 cup	Flour	50 ml
1 tsp.	Cinnamon, ground	5 ml
3 tbsp.	Melted butter	45 ml

Preheat oven to 350°F (180°C). Peel and slice the apples rinse in a salt-water bath and drain well. Mix together sour cream, sugar, flour and eggs, stir well and add vanilla. Fold the drained apples into the sour cream mixture. Place the pastry into an 11 inch (28 cm) pie plate leaving approximately 1 inch (2.5 cm) of pastry over the edge. Fold the 1 inch (2.5 cm) back to form a ridge above the rim of the plate and crimp (this will stop the mixture from spilling over the edge while baking). Pour the filling into the shell. Bake for 30 minutes. While the pie is baking, mix together the Brown Sugar Topping. Remove the pie from the oven and sprinkle the topping evenly over the whole pie, return to the oven and bake for another 30–40 minutes or until the juices run clear.

Serving suggestions: Serve with a cappuccino or a latte.

Linda Crossley & Gerrit Visser, Chefs
Village Cantina

Chocolate Saskatoon Brownie

Yields: 24 squares
Serves: 12

12 oz.	Dark chocolate	375 ml
1 1/2 lbs.	Butter, unsalted	750 g
12	Eggs	12
5 cups	White sugar	1.25 litres
1 cup	Cocoa powder	250 ml
3 cups	Flour	750 ml

Place chocolate and butter in double boiler and melt. Place melted chocolate and butter into a mixer and whisk in eggs and white sugar. Whip for 1 minute and add cocoa powder and flour. Mix until combined. Pour mixture onto a parchment-lined baking sheet and bake for 25 minutes at 325°F (160°C).

Serving suggestions: Cut brownies to 4 x 4 inch (10 x 10 cm) squares. Place 1/2 piece of brownie on a plate. Scoop Saskatoon sorbet (or your favourite fruit-based ice cream) on to the brownie, top with marinated berries of your choice. Place the other half of brownie on top and cover with chocolate syrup. Garnish with fresh mint and serve.

Marinated Berries

1 cup	Seasonal berries	250 ml
1 tbsp.	Sweetener	15 ml

Mix berries with sweetener and let sit for 30 minutes before using. Sugar, honey, maple syrup, Grand Marnier or another liqueur are all suitable sweeteners.

Kelly Gillespie and Dwayne Ennest, Chefs
Diner Deluxe

Texas Style Cheesecake

Serves: 12

Crust

1 1/2 cups	Graham crumbs	375 ml
1/2 cup	Butter, melted	125 ml
1/4 cup	Sugar	50 ml

Filling

3 lbs.	Cream cheese	1.5 kg
3 cups	Sugar	750 ml
3 cups	Sour cream	750 ml
2 tbsp.	Vanilla extract	30 ml
4	Egg yolks	4
8	Egg whites	8

Mix first five filling ingredients until smooth and place into a bowl. Whip egg whites separately and then fold in to mixture. Do not use machine, hand fold only! Mix crust ingredients together separately.

Place two strips of parchment paper in your moulds — 16 oz./500 g onion soup bowls — to make a cross which will hold the cheesecake. Cut a circle the size of the mould, for bottom, to hold graham crust base. Wrap a piece of parchment paper 3 inches (7.5 cm) higher than mould itself. When cheesecakes rise, they will have a wall for support. Set in a water bath, and bake at 275°F (140°C) for approximately 1 1/2 hours.

Jake Kirchner, Executive Chef
Carver's Steakhouse, Sheraton Cavalier

The Living Room's Warm Soft Dark Chocolate Cake

Serves: 8

8 oz.	Bittersweet chocolate (Bernard Callebaut)	250 g
1 cup	Unsalted butter	250 ml
5	Large eggs	5
5	Large egg yolks	5
1 cup	Sugar	250 ml
1 tsp.	Vanilla extract	5 ml
1 cup	Flour	250 ml

Optional: Fresh berries

Place chocolate and butter in a bowl over simmering water and melt completely. Remove from heat and cool slightly. In a large bowl, whisk together eggs, sugar and vanilla. Add a small amount of the chocolate mixture to the egg mixture to temper. Add this to the remaining chocolate mixture and stir well. Fold in flour. Grease and flour eight 5 oz. (150 g) ramekins and fill three quarters full of cake mix. Bake in 425°F (220°C) oven for approximately 12 minutes or until semi-firm to the touch. Allow cakes to rest in ramekins for 2–3 minutes. Run knife around cake to remove. Gently invert ramekins and place on dessert plate.

Serving suggestion: Serve with your favourite fresh berries.

Janice Hepburn, Chef
The Living Room

Grand Marnier and Chocolate Ganache Crème Brûlée

Serves: 8

Ganache

1 cup	Whipping cream	250 ml
1 1/2 cups	Semi-sweet couverture-grade chocolate, broken into pieces	375 g

Bring whipping cream to a boil and pour over chocolate. Stir until lumps are gone. If there are still some bits left, just strain through a sieve. Pour 2 tablespoons (30 ml) of ganache into the bottom of the ramekins and freeze for about 20 minutes.

Crème Brûlée

4 cups	Whipping cream	1 litre
8	Egg yolks	8
4	Whole eggs	4
7 1/2 oz.	Granulated sugar	200 g
2	Oranges, zest	2
2 1/2 oz.	Grand Marnier	75 ml
	Granulated sugar for caramelizing	

Mix egg yolks and whole eggs together. Bring the cream and sugar to a boil. Use a wooden spoon to slowly temper the cream into the yolks (using a spoon helps to avoid too much air being added to the mixture). Strain this mixture.

Add the zest and liqueur. Let cool slightly. Fill the prepared ramekins with the brûlée. Place the ramekins in a baking pan and fill with enough hot water to come halfway up the side of the ramekins. Place a piece of plastic wrap across the top of the baking sheet. This helps to prevent the top from getting too brown during baking. Bake at 325°F (160°C) for about 25 minutes. Let cool and then store in refrigerator until needed. Can be prepared a few days in advance. To finish off, sprinkle top with some granulated sugar and caramelize the top using a propane torch.

Note: The number of brûlée you get from this mix and baking time depends on the size of your ramekins. You need to look for a slightly firm feel without any bubbles on top. Bubbles are a sure sign of being over baked.

Any leftover ganache can be used melted over ice cream or added to hot milk for a hot chocolate. Also, when it is cold, you can scoop little balls to make your own truffles coated in cocoa powder, or icing sugar, or dipped in melted chocolate and rolled in chocolate shavings.

Suzanne Taylor, Pastry Chef
Delta Bow Valley

Bernard Callebaut's Chocolate Pâté
with Raspberry Sauce

Yields: One 8 1/2 x 4 1/2 inch (21 x 10 cm) loaf pan

4 oz.	White chocolate	125 g
4 oz.	Milk chocolate	125 g
4 oz.	Bittersweet chocolate	125 g
3/4 cups	Unsalted butter	150 g
2 cups	Heavy cream (33%)	500 ml

Melt white, milk and bittersweet chocolate separately over a double boiler. Add to each bowl 1/4 cup (50 g) of the unsalted butter. Stir each chocolate until smooth and then take the bowls off the heat to let cool to room temperature. In a chilled bowl, use a chilled whisk and beat the heavy cream until soft peaks form. Using a rubber spatula, fold one third of the whipped cream into each type of chocolate. Dark chocolate tends to harden quicker, so be sure it doesn't cool too much before mixing with whipped cream.

Put a layer of plastic wrap in the bottom of a loaf pan. Spoon the white chocolate mixture into the bottom of the pan. Then layer the milk chocolate mixture and spread evenly. Then layer the bittersweet chocolate mixture and spread evenly. Cover with plastic wrap and refrigerate for at least 2 hours. Remove the pâté from the refrigerator 2 hours before serving, but do not unwrap the plastic cover until the mixture reaches room temperature.

Assembly of dish: Cut the slices 1/2 inch (12 mm) thick, place on a dessert plate and add 2–3 tablespoons (30–45 ml) of the raspberry sauce (see below). Pâté can be made in advance and stored in the refrigerator or frozen either whole or in individual slices.

Raspberry Sauce

3 pints	Raspberries, fresh **or** frozen	1.7 litres

Purée raspberries in a blender. Pour into a heavy saucepan and reduce to half its volume. Cool down in the refrigerator. Any leftover raspberry sauce can be frozen.

Bernard Callebaut, Chocolatier

White Chocolate and Huckleberry Crème Brûlée

Serves: 8

Huckleberry Juice

1 cup	Sugar	250 ml
1/4 cup	Water	50 ml
4 cups	Huckleberries	1 litre
1	Lemon, zest	1

Make sugar water, add huckleberries and zest, simmer for 1 hour.

Crème Brûlée

6 cups	Heavy cream	1.5 litres
1 1/2 cups	Sugar	375 ml
1	Vanilla bean, split	1
9 oz	White chocolate, finely chopped	250 g
15	Egg yolks	15
1/2 cup	Huckleberry juice	125 ml

In a saucepan heat cream, sugar and vanilla over medium–high heat and bring to a boil. Remove from heat and stir in chocolate until melted. In a bowl, whisk egg yolks until frothy and slowly add cream mixture.

Add huckleberry juice and strain. Put in fridge and allow to set overnight. If baking custards that day, skim foam off the top of mixture. Fill ramekins and put them in a baking pan with warm water halfway up the sides of the ramekins and bake at 300°F (150°C) covered with foil for 30 minutes. Remove foil, check and bake until set. Remove from water to cool.

Possible substitutions for huckleberries: blueberries, blackberries, strawberries

Randy Hollands, Executive Chef
The Ranche Restaurant

Smuggler's Ginger Spice Bars

Yields: 40 bars

1/2 cup	Butter	125 ml
1 cup	Granulated sugar	250 ml
1	Egg	1
1/3 cup	Molasses	75 ml
1 tsp.	Baking soda	5 ml
1 tsp.	Cinnamon, ground	5 ml
2 tsp.	Ginger, ground	10 ml
1/2 tsp.	Cloves, ground	2 ml
1/2 cup	Raisins	125 ml
1/4 cup	Dried cranberries (optional)	60 ml
1 tbsp.	Crystallized ginger, chopped	15 ml
2 cups	All purpose flour	500 ml
	Sugar, to sprinkle on top	

Preheat oven to 375°F (190°C). Cream butter and sugar. Beat in eggs, molasses, baking soda and spices. Stir in fruit. Gradually incorporate flour until dough is very stiff. On lightly floured surface take a quarter of the dough at a time and shape into 12-inch (30 cm) logs. Bake 12 minutes on lightly greased cookie sheet or until lightly browned. (Be careful not to over bake as top will not change much in colour.) Sprinkle with sugar while top is still hot. Cut in to bars.

Note: These will keep well in the freezer.

Michael Atwell, Pastry Chef
Smuggler's Inn

Sticky Gingerbread Pudding

Yields: 6 squares

1/2 cup	Butter	125 ml
1/2 cup	Brown sugar	125 ml
1/2 cup	Molasses	125 ml
1/2 cup	Corn syrup	125 ml
2 tbsp.	Ginger, ground	30 ml
1 tsp.	Cinnamon, ground	5 ml
1 tsp.	Nutmeg	5 ml
1/4 cup	Sweet sherry	50 ml
1/2 cup	Milk, warmed	125 ml
3	Eggs, beaten	3
1 1/2 cups	Flour	375 ml
1	Orange, juiced and grated rind	1
1/2 cup	Sultanas	125 ml

Cream together butter and sugar. Add molasses, syrup, spices, sherry and milk. Stir well until mixed. Alternately add eggs, flour, orange juice and grated orange rind plus sultanas and beat well. Pour mixture into a well-greased 12 x 9 inch (30 x 20 cm) baking tin and bake at 350°F (180°C) for 45 minutes.

Remove from pan and let cool on a wire rack. Cut in to squares and serve with whipped cream and caramel sauce (e.g. Smiths canned sauce).

Garry Hennessey, Chef
Open Sesame

Bernard Callebaut's Chocolate Martini

Serves: 4

3 oz.	Brandy	90 ml
3 oz	Crème de cacao	90 ml
2 oz.	Cream	60 ml
1/2 oz.	Semi-sweet or bittersweet Bernard Callebaut chocolate, chopped	15 ml
to taste	Nutmeg, grated/ground	to taste

Heat cream and finely chopped chocolate in a small saucepan on low heat. Stirring constantly, simmer until the chocolate is melted and blended with the cream. Put saucepan in cold water to reduce the temperature of the mixture, while continuing to stir. Pour liqueur into a martini shaker and add the chocolate mixture with crushed ice. Shake, then strain into chilled cocktail glasses. Dust with nutmeg.

Bernard Callebaut, Chocolatier

Moroccan Mint Tea

Serves: 4–6

3–4 tbsp.	Sugar	45–60 ml
1/2–1 tsp.	Orange blossom water	2–5ml
1–2 tbsp.	**or** dried orange blossoms	15–30 ml
1/2–1 tsp.	China green tea (Special Gunpowder)	2–5ml
bunch	Fresh mint (spearmint or peppermint) Boiling water	bunch

In a tea pot, preferably silver, add sugar and sprinkle with orange blossom water or dried orange blossoms and the China Green Tea (Special Gunpowder is green tea leaves rolled in tight small balls). Add a generous handful of fresh mint. Fill pot with boiling water, stir well and serve in small tea glasses to round off a meal.

Orange blossom water: Available at Cretan or Arabic groceteria; look for green tea at Chinese stores.

Ismaili Houssine, Chef
Sultan's Tent

Restaurants

Aida's

From the heart of Lebanon to your hearth and home, Aida shares the magic of a healthy, light cuisine. Since its debut two years ago Aida's has received such awards as "Best New Restaurant 2000," has been rated 9 out of 10 by CBC Radio's John Gilchrist, and Where Magazine has given the restaurant "Rising Star Award 2000" and the "Most Memorable Meal" award. Fast Forward gave the restaurant "Best International 2000 Award." But its strongest accolades come from the streams of regular patrons who keep the 40-seat restaurant full. There is eastern magic in the air at Aida's and the walls are filled with the owner's daughter's photographs of Lebanon. The kitchen is filled with women, all of Lebanese descent, whose love and authenticity is present in everything Aida serves and is felt by everyone who enters the restaurant.

Mon 11am–9pm, Tues–Thurs, 11am–10pm, Fri & Sat, 11am–11pm, Sun, 4pm–9pm • 541–1189 • 2208–4th Street SW

Cannery Row & McQueens Upstairs

Cannery Row & McQueens Upstairs offer the best choices for both casual and fine dining. Cannery Row is Calgary's first oyster bar. With its casual Cajun atmosphere, it features the best seafood menu Calgary has to offer. Specialties include live Atlantic lobster, West Coast Dungeness crab and Malpeque oysters, to jambalaya and a large selection of fresh fish flown in from all over the world. Our new and exciting award winning Executive Chef, John Skinner, brings a wealth of culinary knowledge and flair to both restaurants. Decorated in a Chicago speakeasy style, McQueens Upstairs is an exceptionally comfortable restaurant. It offers everything from seafood and Alberta beef to wild game. Every dish you find in both restaurants is an extension of John's personality and flair.

Cannery Row: Mon–Fri, 11:00am–2pm, Open for dinner 7 days a week • 269–8889
McQueens Upstairs: Tues–Sat, 5:30pm–closing • 269–4722
- 317–10th Avenue SW
- www.canneryrowrestaurant.com

Cilantro Restaurant

Cilantro is a 75-seat rustic style restaurant, with an additional 55-seat enclosed patio and veranda. The veranda is surrounded by candle light and luscious Virginia creepers giving the cozy and quaint atmosphere the restaurant has been known for since 1988. It is the winner of many "Nest Patio" awards. Chef Ken Canavan is the creator of the menu, which has an unconventional California–Southwestern flair. In addition the restaurant offers daily and nightly features with the specialties being flat-bread style pizzas, home-made pastas along with many different appetizers, salads and entrées; something to suit everyone's tastes! Cilantro's offers an extensive wine list and feature up to 25 different wines by the glass. We are proud to be a recipient of the Wine Spectator's "Award of Excellence" for their list from 1996 through 2001.

Sun 5pm–10pm, Mon–Thurs, 11am–11pm, Fri, 11am–12pm, Sat 5pm–12pm • 229–1177
- 338–17th Avenue SW

Diner Deluxe

Serving up a good breakfast in this town had always been something Dwayne and Alberta had talked about doing. Fortunately for them, the diner just "materialized" one day. A friend of Alberta's family had done an amazing job renovating an old coffee shop and was looking to sell the restaurant as a more or less turnkey operation. An easy to miss "hole in the wall" from the street, inside the decor is a real trip back into mom's kitchen in the 1950's, complete with Formica chrome tables and space age lamps. The menu Dwayne created is a fun change of pace from his fine-dining past, and his simple old-fashioned diner fare is something everyone can relate to and enjoy. Longtime Calgary chef Dwayne Ennest apprenticed for six years under Austrian chef Herbert Obrect, and learned while he travelled internationally. He worked his way up to Day Chef at Teatro, was chef at Mescalero and then at the River Café on Princes Island Park. Now an owner and chef of the Diner Deluxe, he looks forward to opening his own 18-seat fine-dining room, Supperclub, next door to Diner Deluxe.

Mon–Fri, 7:30am–9:30pm, Sat 8:00am–3:00pm and 5:00pm–9:30pm, Sun 8:00am–3:00p • 276–5499
- 804 Edmonton Trail NE

Il Sogno

Chef/Co-owner Giuseppe Di Gennaro of Il Sogno passionately re-introduces Italian cuisine to North Americans through the traditions of Napoli. Using the finest imported ingredients available, he brings his passion to life through presentation, flavour and flair. Giuseppe has gathered skill and experience preparing and serving internationally in Italy, London and Australia. He chose Calgary as his new home just four years ago, the place to make his dream a reality. Il Sogno is celebrating its second anniversary in 2002.

Lunch Tues–Fri, 11:30am–2pm, dinner Tues–Sun, 5pm–9pm, Sunday brunch 10:30am–2pm, closed Mondays
- 232–8901 • 24–4th Street NE
- www.ilsogno.org

Westin Hotel: Owl's Nest

Martin Heusser, Executive Chef at the Westin Hotel, Calgary and the Owl's Nest, is the leader of a culinary team that produces award- winning and memorable meals. He likes to use organic products and pairs them with sauces that enhance the natural flavours of the food. The multitude of colourful and light styles of West Coast cuisine inspires him and he delights in integrating them with his strong background in continental cuisine. Martin, following a family tradition of creative cuisine, is originally from Bann, Germany. Enroute to the Owl's Nest at the Westin in Calgary, he trained and worked in Germany, Sweden, Vancouver and Whistler. He has cooked for Kings, Queens, Nobel Laureates and many satisfied guests.

Mon–Fri, 11:30–2pm, Mon–Sat, 5:30–10:30pm • 508–5164
- 320–4 Avenue SW
- www.westin.com

The Pickled Parrot

The Pickled Parrot opened its doors in July 2002, but it already has a history. The owner, Brendan Glass, has consulted for many of Calgary's top restaurants and bars. The Parrot is a casual spot to relax with fabulous food, great beers and wines. Wine is just one of Brendan's passions. He is a member of Les Chevalier Des Vin De France. Executive Chef, William Beaton and Associate Chef, Michelle Ducie, run the Parrot's kitchen. Both have worked in some of Calgary's best restaurants; Bonterra and Florentines to name a few. The menu is based on British pub fair, cooked to perfection with a creative and contemporary twist. (Continued on following page)

Pub: Mon–Sat 11:30am–2:30am
Kitchen: Mon–Wed,
11:30am–11pm, Thurs–Sat,
11:30am–12am, closed Sundays
- 229–2090
- 501–17th Avenue SW

Teatro Restaurant

Teatro, one of Calgary's finest and favourite restaurants, is home to Executive Chef Michael Allemeier. Chef Allemeier is known for his many accolades and most recently as host on the hit show "Cook Like a Chef." Michael's extensive training and experience throughout Western Canada brought him to Teatro five years ago. The Teatro menu is a rich feast of flavour using only the finest ingredients available. Teatro is situated in the historic Dominion Bank in the arts district of Calgary. Teatro is proud of its award-winning cellar housed in the old bank vaults.

Mon–Thurs, 11:30am–11pm, Fri,
11:30am–midnight,
Sat, 5pm–midnight, Sun, 5pm–10pm
- 290–1012 • 200 Stephen
Avenue Walk (8th Avenue) SE
- www.teatro–rest.com

Thai-Sa-On

Thai-Sa-On is certified by Thailand's Ministry of Commerce, and John Gilchrist, CBC Radio's food critic, rates it "consistently the best Thai food in Calgary." This is a family run restaurant. Mother Vanh is the Head Chef, sisters Sonthaya, Vida and Auntie Kalayarat are the assistant chefs. The other family members are the hosts. Serving strictly Thai food, Thai-Sa-On's specialty is authentic royal Thai cuisine, presenting balanced flavours and spicing. It is all freshly prepared everyday, just like at home. Tom Yam and Yam Nua are two popular dishes and Mother Vanh is famous for her fresh curries, peanut sauce and chili paste. Jackie Chan called this Yam Nua the "Mama Beef."

He dined at Thai-Sa-On twice a week while in Calgary filming Shanghai Noon.

Mon–Fri, 11:30–2pm, Mon–Thurs,
5pm–9:30pm, Fri & Sat 5pm–10:30pm
- 254–3526
- 351–10th Avenue SW

The King & I

The King & I was the first restaurant to introduce Thai food to Calgary. Since 1988 this upscale Thai dining room has been serving signature dishes including satays, curries and an ever-changing series of special dishes. "Designed" is the operative word at The King and I. Winner of numerous awards, The King & I offers a beautiful, stylish series of elegant and contemporary dining rooms with superb ambience. The setting, which is conducive to lingering over dinner, the service and the unique, delectable dishes, combine to create an evening that shouldn't be missed by anyone appreciative of fine cuisine.

Mon–Thurs, 11:30am–10:30pm, Fri,
11:30am–11:30pm Sat,
4:30–11:30pm, Sun, 4:30–10:30pm
- 264–7241
- 822–11th Avenue SW

River Café

River Café is located in the middle of Prince's Island Park on the lagoon where the Bow River passes through downtown Calgary. The beautiful, tranquil setting is accessed only by pedestrian traffic. The culinary focus is Canadian regional wood–fired cuisine. Chef Glen Manzer seeks out the best of the Northwest, serving organic and free-range products from local suppliers and from the River Café garden. With its accomplished cuisine and panoramic views of the park and the dramatic cityscape beyond, River Café has established itself as a Western Canadian culinary destination. (Continued on following page)

Mon–Fri, 11:00–11pm, Sat–Sun,
10:00–11pm, closed all January
• 261-7670 • Prince's Island
Park • www.river-cafe.com

The Village Cantina

It started with pies. In 1996 Linda Crossley and Gerrit Visser opened their doors with delicious homemade pies. Soon people were coming to feast on treats and visit "the birds," Dick and Bert, tropical residents at the Cantina. The mother and son team has been a staple at the Creative Living Kitchen Theatre (at the Calgary Stampede) for six consecutive years. Their hospitality and savoury food are the heart of The Village Cantina, offering international casual cuisine...and designer pies!

Tues–Fri, 11am–10pm, Sat–Sun,
10am–3pm, Sat evening show time,
7pm–midnight • 265-5739
• 1413–9th Avenue SE

Wildwood

Executive Chef Josef Wiewer and his team have created and defined Western Canadian cuisine. In the tastefully refined Wildwood dining room, the menu features local ingredients and offers any number of regional dishes including elk, caribou and buffalo or Calgary's very best lamb burger. All combined with a sophistication that reflects Josef's international culinary experience while celebrating Alberta's culture and cuisine. There are other options at Wildwood, as there is a fabulous deck to enjoy, as well as the onsite brew pub.

Mon–Thurs, 11:30am–10pm, Fri and
Sat 11:30am–11pm, Sun 5pm–10pm
• 288-0100
• 2417–4th Street SW
• www.creativeri.com

4th Street Rose

4th Street Rose is proud to be the only restaurant in Calgary serving a 100%-dedicated Californian food and wine menu. They have even gone as far as to fly in Californian winery chefs every three weeks to create and innovate dazzling cuisine and pair it with amazing wines. General Manager, David Singleton and Executive Chef, Stephen Little bring over 30 years combined experience in the restaurant trade. The 4th St. Rose has Calgary's best people-watching patio set in the heart of the dining district. As well, they also have a little-known secret, the private dining room located above the main floor dining room. It boasts a more intimate setting complete with a two-sided fire place, sky light, a view of 4th Street and cool music. 4th Street Rose has received numerous accolades such as "Best Bistro" from The Straight, "Best Café" from Where Magazine and many editorial reviews of their new menu, its style and commitment to delicious cuisine, as well as their overall polished service.

Mon–Fri 11–1am, Sat 10–1am, Sun
10–11pm • 228-5377
• 2116–4th Street SW

Bernard Callebaut

Growing up in Belgium, Bernard Callebaut was destined to become a chocolatier. It was in the town of Wieze, Belgium that he nurtured a passion for chocolate — with his roots in the then family-owned Callebaut Chocolate Factory. From 1911 to 1980, the established enterprise produced some of Europe's finest chocolates. Eventually sold to Suchard Toblerone, the factory prospered in the production of over 77 million pounds of bulk chocolate every year. Notably, he is the first Callebaut to pioneer the creation of individual handmade chocolates for which he has received international recognition and awards. In 1998, he was awarded the title of (Continued on following page)

"Grand Prix International Artisan Chocolatier" in the international Festival of Chocolate in Roanne, France. With dedication to quality and innovative craftsmanship, he is also renowned for his unique style of chocolate fillings. In 1982, he had a vision: to offer North Americans the same superior chocolates Europe had been enjoying for years. His philosophy is simple. By using only the purest ingredients and uncompromising quality, North America can experience "chocolate enlightenment."

Head office: 265–5777 / 800 661–8367 • 1313–1st Street SE
• www.bernardcallebaut.com

Big Rock Grill

The Big Rock Grill is on-site at the Big Rock Brewery. The restaurant specializes in rotisserie dishes and European cuisine. Combine a brewing process tour with a tasty lunch. The Big Rock grill is also available for evening bookings of dinner and party groups, special events, weddings and banquets for up to 100 guests.

Mon–Fri 11–3pm • 236–1606
• 5555–76th Avenue SE
• www.bigrockbeer.com

Dante's Restaurant & Tapas & Wine Bar

Enjoy quick and pleasant service at this cozy downtown spot. Located in Penny Lane Mall, it is perfect for power lunches. The menu features a wide variety of specially prepared continental foods in keeping with healthy eating trends. There are many classics on the menu from smoked salmon and seafood chowder to chicken, venison and lamb. The wine bar features a tapas menu for those who prefer a more casual setting.

Mon 11am–5pm, Tue–Fri 11am–11pm, Sat 5–11pm • 237–5787
• 210, 513–8th Avenue SW

Delta Bow Valley: The Conservatory

Quaint, welcoming and intimate best describes the charm and atmosphere of The Conservatory which is recognized for a fine, innovative cuisine and superb in-house desserts. Central to the dining room is the table d'hote menu, designed weekly to feature seasonal and local specialties. The combination of creative culinary talent and impeccable service provides the harmony for The Conservatory dining experience.

Tue–Sat 5:30–10pm • 266–1980
• 209–4th Avenue SE
• www.deltahotels.com

Fleur de Sel

Fleur de Sel is located in the Tivoli building, a former movie theater. It still features the original high ceilings and a portion of an uncovered brick wall. The long, curved counter or "comptoir" winds towards the open kitchen. If you like pop art, you'll recognize the "Calder Waves" painting, visible from every seat. The light jazz allows for intimate conversations. Step in to a small restaurant and enjoy French cuisine in a brasserie setting. The menu is filled with unexpected pleasures, combining tradition with nouveau. Owner Patrice Durandeau and his team, Chef Dan McKinley and Maitre D' Dale Bremer show their passion for food and wine.

Summer: lunch Tue–Fri, dinner Tue–Sunday
Winter: lunch Tues–Fri, dinner Mon–Sun, "open until the last guests"
• Reservations 228–9764
• 2015–4th Street SW

La Chaumière Restaurant

La Chaumière Restaurant serves French market cuisine in an elegant dining room or comfortable patio overlooking Rouleauville Square. Executive Chef C.R. Matthews prepares an imaginative menu with entrées such as Ahi Tuna with Seafood Brandade, Veal Medallions and Foie Gras with Madeira Sauce. The extensive wine list has 750 selections from around the world. La Chaumière Restaurant also features a variety of private rooms capable of providing boutique banquets for up to 100 people.

Mon–Fri 11:45am–2:30pm,
5:45–midnight, Sat 5:30–midnight
- 228–5690
- 139–17th Avenue SW
- www.lachaumiere.ca

Open Sesame

Open Sesame is an adventure in fresh Asian dining. The restaurant features dramatic award-winning décor with lots of nooks and private spaces. Guests are encouraged to create their own stir-fry from the market garden and watch as the wok chefs skillfully cook up a masterpiece. There is also an extensive menu with appetizers such as Salt and Pepper Prawns, Chinese Chicken in Lettuce Cups, as well as main courses such as Ginger Beef, Dragon Noodles, or Buddah's Bowl. Don't forget to save some room for Banana Wontons and Chocolate Spring Rolls for dessert!

Mon–Sat 11:30am–11pm, Sunday
4:30–10pm • 259–0123
- 6920 Macleod Trail South
- www.open-sesame.tv

Sheraton Cavalier: Carver's Steakhouse

The number one steakhouse in Calgary, the ambiance of Carver's Steakhouse delights the eye with modern art and a warm décor, enhanced by impeccable service. Carver's Steakhouse was designed to embrace and showcase the finest beef the province of Alberta has to offer. Contemporary design and furniture make Carver's an excellent location to meet colleagues and friends. Readers of Where Magazine awarded Carver's Steakhouse the "Steakhouse of the Year" in 1999 and "Restaurant of the Year" in 2000.

Mon–Sat 5:30–10:30 pm, Sun 5–9pm
- 250–6327 • 2620–32 Ave. NE
- www.sheraton-calgary.com

Smuggler's Inn

Smuggler's Inn has been one of the biggest and busiest restaurants in Calgary for over 30 years. Its claim to fame is its prime rib, slowly roasted in special ovens, but the menu also includes great Alberta steaks, chicken and fish. All meals include a bountiful soup and salad bar (don't miss the Portuguese Bean and Sausage Soup). The atmosphere is cozy and comfortable, with high back chairs, lots of woodwork and numerous fireplaces. Smuggler's is a Calgary landmark restaurant, a favourite of the locals and the ranchers of the region.

Mon–Sat 11:30am–11 pm, Sunday
brunch 10–2, dinner 4:30–10pm
- 252–3394
- 6920 Macleod Trail South
- www.smugglers-inn.com

Sultan's Tent

Moroccan cuisine is generally hidden from the world and rarely served in local restaurants. It combines gentle, subtle spices such as saffron, ginger, cumin and paprika to create delicious and refined dishes such as tagines or "stews" of vegetables and chicken, lamb, fish, cornish hen or rabbit. Couscous, a platter of steamed wheat grains served with meat and seven vegetables, is a Moroccan cultural staple that is tasty, filling and (Continued on following page) nutritious. Ismaili Houssine, chef at Sultan's Tent, is a master of the cuisine and personally oversees each dish. Owners Coby, Jackie and Martin are pleased to invite guests to enjoy the Sultan's Tent cuisine in an authentic traditional ambience evocative of the rich heritage of Morocco.

Mon–Fri, 5:30–11:00pm, Sat, 5:00–11:00pm • 244-2333
• 909–17th Avenue SW

The Fairmont Palliser: The Rimrock

The Rimrock has long been known as the place for special occasions and the best prime rib in town. This is classic dining revitalized. Great food and attentive service in a beautiful atmosphere — without the formality. Creative appetizers, succulent cuts of beef and decadent house-made desserts are served in this downtown restaurant.

Breakfast Mon–Sat 6:30–11am; Sun 7–11am; Lunch, Sun–Fri 11am–2pm, Dinner, 5:30–10pm
• Reservations 260–1219
• 133–9th Avenue SW

The Living Room

The Living Room has coined the term "contemporary interactive cuisine" to describe their philosophy. This is defined as an expanded twist on classical cuisine with heavy French and Italian influence. The menu includes traditional cheese, meat and chocolate fondue, roasted chicken, Porterhouse steak, crêpes and bouillabaisse. The restaurant prides itself on an extensive tapas list with a diverse selection of entrées and daily features of outstanding meats, fish and seafood.

Mon–Fri 11:30am–2am, Sat 5pm–2am, Sun 5pm–midnight • 228-9830
• 514–17th Avenue SW
• www.letsgofordinner.com

The Ranche Restaurant at Fish Creek Provincial Park

This spectacular historic site lies nestled in a serene meadow less than 20 minutes from downtown Calgary. The Bow Valley Ranche at the east end of Fish Creek Provincial Park stands as a reminder of Calgary's rich ranching heritage. Originally built in 1896 by William Roper Hull and later purchased by ranching tycoon Senator Patrick Burns, it has been owned by the Province of Alberta since 1973. Through the efforts of The Ranche at Fish Creek Restoration Society, these wonderful buildings are once again a grand country estate for the enjoyment of all and serve as a meeting place for business, social and family gatherings. Dining facilities include rooms that seat from 12 to 100 people.

Mon–Thur 11:30am–9:00pm, Fri 11:30am–10:00pm, Sat 5:00–10:00pm, Sun 10:30am–9:00pm • 255-3939
• 15979 Bow Bottom Trail SE
• www.theranche.com

Index

About the Editors

Myriam Leighton is a published writer who co-authored the original book in this series. She is an avid gardener and naturalist who like her co-author, Jennifer Stead, loves to experiment and be creative in her kitchen. Jennifer Stead is a professional artist and educator who gardens and cooks with pleasure.